have your cake
and **vegan too**

have your cake
and **vegan too**

50 Dazzling and Delicious
Cake Creations

••• **KRIS HOLECHEK**

Ulysses Press

Published by:
Ulysses Press
P.O. Box 3440
Berkeley, CA 94703
www.ulyssespress.com

ISBN: 978-1-56975-920-2
Library of Congress Catalog Number 2011921434

Printed in the United States by Bang Printing

10 9 8 7 6 5 4 3 2 1

Acquisitions editor: Kelly Reed
Managing editor: Claire Chun
Editor: Leslie Evans
Proofreader: Lauren Harrison
Index: Sayre Van Young
Photography: © Kris Holechek
Design and layout: what!design @ whatweb.com
Production: Judith Metzener

Distributed by Publishers Group West

To Trisha Mikelonis, for teaching me the joy of serving good food to my loved ones. And for Marlene Gaige, for teaching me to make my own opportunities.

CONTENTS

Chapter 4

Chapter 5

Chapter 6

Chapter 7

ACKNOWLEDGMENTS

A big thank you and mad props to all of my loyal testers: Lynda Bascelli, Courtney Blair, Katie Bolt, Smyth Campbell, Jamie Coble, Erica DeCouteau, Aimee Kluiber, Amie Kolesar, Ana Lucas, Clea Mahoney, Karen Mallonee, Karie Miller, Maggie Muggins, Meghan-Rose O'Neill, Josiane Richer, Marcia Torpey, Molly Walter, and Soozie Zawistowski. Your hard work and troubleshooting efforts were greatly appreciated. A special shout out to super-tester Lee Ann Light, who not only tested almost every single recipe but also suggested two of the more unique recipes to make the cut.

Thanks to all of my blog readers and the readers and users of my previous books. Your encouragement and feedback are always appreciated and I truly value you. Getting to know you and share the gift of delicious vegan food has been one of the greatest joys of my life.

Of course, special thanks to my friends and family, my lovely and crazy-making kittehs, and especially my husband, Jim. I owe you a lifetime of gratitude for all of the buttercream-bowl-washing, scraping-frosting-off-the-ceiling, late-night-running-for-ingredients, sweeping-up-flour, and-whatever-else goodness you provided. Your love and support, along with your endless stomach and capacity for taste testing, are priceless.

What is a cake?

Yes, I'm going to wax poetic about cake. What can I say—it's been on my mind quite a bit lately.

Some say that unless it's got two layers and is smothered in frosting, it's not a cake. Others eschew tradition and say that the line-crossing cheesecake is fully cemented in cakehood. Still others couldn't care less, so long as they get a slice.

In working on this collection of recipes, I thought a lot about cake. It would have been easy to whip up a basic cake recipe and replay it fifty times, with a slight variance of flavors and add-ins, but that's not my style. Within these pages, expect to have your own definition of cake challenged and expanded. Single-layer cakes. Double-layer cakes. Coffee and crumb cakes. Snack cakes. Upside-down cakes. Cakes without topping or icing. Cakes that don't even require an oven! And if you've ever doubted the ability to make a tasty cake without eggs, butter, or milk, think again. These pages contain the keys to the vegan cake kingdom, unlocking moist, fluffy cakes with a tender crumb and more toppings than you can shake a stick at, plus plenty of options for our gluten-free friends.

The unifying factors to all of these recipes is that they are cruelty-free and delicious and provide options for every cake-consuming opportunity in life: fancy cake events (birthdays, showers, weddings), more casual events (dinner parties and afternoon visits), and everyday eating (morning, noon, and night). One major thing to love about cakes is their versatility. Cake is the shape-shifter of baked goods—it can morph from one form to the next within the blink of an eye (or just a different kind of pan!).

If you're new to the land of cakes, never fear. The sheer beauty of a cake is almost to its detriment. They seem overwhelming and labor intensive, which is quite the opposite of the truth. In fact, cakes are so simple that once you make a couple you'll shake your head and wonder, "Why did I think this would be so hard?" And then you'll sit down and eat some more cake!

Whether you split a slice with family or bring half a coffee cake to cheer up a friend, the act of sharing cake is such an ancient way of connecting, it's akin to breaking bread. A slice of moist, delectable cake is a sure way to put some pep in your step and spread that joy to those around you.

I hope you and yours enjoy these recipes.

Happy Baking,
Kris

CAKE MAKING TOOLS

Here are some tools for your arsenal that are essential for cake-baking perfection.

Pans As basic as it gets, your pan is your first line of defense against bad cakes. Metal pans are best for baking as metal distributes heat most evenly. Purchase pans without nonstick, when possible. Nonstick coating browns the outer part of a cake too quickly and with darker cakes can actually burn them. Glass pans are a good second choice, if you don't have metal pans available. I do not use or recommend silicone bakeware. It's very easy to tear your cake, they bake less evenly, and frankly they haven't been around long enough for me to believe that they are safe. Look at what we're learning about nonstick coating thirty years later. I understand their fat-free appeal, but seriously? We're baking cakes, and a light pan greasing isn't going to make or break it.

Here are the basic pans you should have to seamlessly navigate the land of cakes:

- **8-INCH ROUND PAN** Having two of these is optimal, as it makes baking layer cakes easier. Not only does baking each layer in a separate pan make filling and stacking them a breeze, they bake up better than one round full of batter. You can use 9-inch rounds instead, but you will need to be mindful of your baking time and decrease it by a few minutes because the layers will be thinner.

- **8-INCH SQUARE PAN** This size pan is perfect for coffee cakes. It is problematic to find in metal, but you can use a glass pan instead. An 9-inch square pan can also be used, but the baking time may decrease by a few minutes because the layer will be thinner.

- **9 X 13-INCH PAN** This is the standard size you see for many "sheet cakes," when in fact it is actually a quarter of the size of a sheet cake from a professional bakery, so keep that in mind if you ever order one! This size pan is great if you want to make a square double-layer cake, too, as you can just cut it in half and stack.

- **8- OR 9-INCH SPRINGFORM PAN** Springform pans have removable sides, which is perfect for cakes that are more delicate or can't be flipped, such as cheesecakes, crumb cakes, or anything else with a topping or delicate texture. Having one trusty springform pan will make your life much easier.

🍂 LOAF PAN   These are typically 9 x 5 inches and are fabulous for pound cakes. Try to find one with vertical sides, rather than tapered, to make fun layered loaf cakes.

🍂 BUNDT PAN   A standard Bundt pan holds 15 cups and is 10 inches in diameter. While the Bundt is the most recognizable shape, they are interchangeable with other tube pans of similar volume. Bundt pans bake pretty cakes that require minimal decoration and help us think outside the square or traditional round.

🍂 JELLY ROLL PAN   Meant for baking very flat, thin cakes, these are typically 10 x 15 inches and have a short lip. While not a necessary tool of the trade, they are quite handy.

🍂 ELECTRIC HANDHELD OR STAND MIXER   Over-beating cake batter is your worst enemy. Using an electric mixer is efficient and helps prevent overbeating. While using a whisk or spatula is technically fine, an electric mixer is recommended for most of these recipes. It is also essential in creating smooth, creamy frosting with no lumps.

🍂 PARCHMENT PAPER   A cousin to waxed paper, although not interchangeable, parchment paper can withstand the high temperatures of an oven and is used to line pans to make removing cakes easier and less messy. It is essential to ensure success with certain baked goods, like upside-down cakes or cakes with more delicate textures.

🍂 SIFTER   Both powdered sugar and baking cocoa get very lumpy, so a sifter is essential for getting those lumps out. Sifting your flour (after measuring) also makes for a fluffier cake.

🍂 RACKS   A basic staple, cooling racks are used for cooling cakes and other baked goods. Placing a hot pan on hot pads or the top of your oven traps the heat on the bottom, causing cakes to cool slowly and unevenly. Having at least two racks is also helpful when you invert a cake out of the pan and then flip it right side up again.

🍂 THERMOMETER   Does this seem like overkill? You'd be surprised. For example, I have a very trusty, newer oven. Yet, when it says it's preheated it actually has about 50°F to go. And when I need to bake something at 375°F, I need to set it for 365°F. A thermometer is a cheap investment to ensure your baked goods are in the right environment.

🍂 PROCESSOR OR BLENDER   Some recipes call for pureeing. A food processor is optimal, but a quality blender can work, too.

CONVERSIONS		
MEASURE	EQUIVALENT	METRIC
1 teaspoon	-----	5 milliliters
1 tablespoon	3 teaspoons	14.8 milliliters
1 cup	16 tablespoons	236.8 milliliters
1 pint	2 cups	473.6 milliliters
1 quart	4 cups	947.2 milliliters
1 liter	4 cups + 3½ tablespoons	1000 milliliters
1 ounce (dry)	-----	28.35 grams
1 pound	16 ounces	453.49 grams
2.21 pounds	35.3 ounces	1 kilogram

VEGAN BAKING: THE 411

Okay, so we're going to bake a bunch of cakes—from classics to zany new creations—and we're not using eggs? We're going to make creamy, fluffy buttercream without butter? We're going to make cheesecake without cheese . . . what?! Yes, I am here to tell you not only will all your recipes be animal-free, they'll be delicious as well. Delicate crumbs. Mouthwatering flavors. Creamy toppings. Your finicky friends and family will never know the difference, and your food will be that much more enjoyable, knowing that you're eating animal-friendly.

REPLACING EGGS

Eggs provide moisture, structure, and texture in baked goods. There are many different ways to get around eggs, ranging from applesauce to soy yogurt to flaxseed. When creating a recipe, my goal is to figure out what eggs would normally do for that sort of cake and then formulate my ingredient list accordingly. Here are the tricks you'll most commonly see in this book:

UNSWEETENED APPLESAUCE Perfect for cakes, applesauce's fibrous nature provides some structure while retaining moisture. It's used in such small quantities that you can't taste it.

VINEGAR By reacting with other elements in a cake (curdling soy milk, activating baking soda, and performing the gastronomical two-step

with cocoa powder), vinegar adds lift to cakes and it locks in moisture. Be sure to use a mild vinegar such as white distilled or apple cider to ensure there is no aftertaste.

SILKEN TOFU This usually comes in a little aseptic cardboard box, although occasionally you may find it water-packed. The little boxes are shelf stable, so you might find silken tofu in the Asian foods section of your grocery store, although some markets do refrigerate it. It's much creamier than the traditional water-packed tofu, but if it's hard to find, soft water-packed tofu can work in a pinch but might require a bit more blending to make it smooth.

. . . .

If you have some nonvegan recipes you'd like to veganize, on page 6 is a handy chart to help

EGG REPLACER	AMOUNT TO USE TO REPLACE 1 EGG	WHERE IT WORKS BEST
Unsweetened applesauce	1/4 cup	Quick breads, muffins, cakes, bars, and cookies
Plain or vanilla soy yogurt	1/4 cup	Cakes, bars, quick breads, and muffins
Ground flaxseed	1 tablespoon flaxseed plus 3 tablespoons water, whipped up and then let to set for a few minutes (it becomes thick like an egg white)	Great for baked goods that are chewy, such as brownies and cookies, and also in yeasted breads, especially sweet ones
Silken tofu	1/4 cup, pureed	Cakes which are slightly dense in texture, pies, quick breads, and muffins
"Sour" milk	1/4 teaspoon mild vinegar (white or apple cider) plus enough milk to make 1/4 cup	Cakes, muffins, and quick breads; works as a hybrid leavening and binder, making things rise and stay moist
Various fruits or vegetables, pureed or shredded, such as canned pumpkin, mashed banana, zucchini, carrots, or pears	1/4 cup	Muffins, quick breads, cakes, and brownies
Milk	1 tablespoon	If a pureed or shredded fruit or vegetable is already in the recipe, you can typically substitute milk for the eggs
Ener-G egg replacer	See directions on box	This boxed replacer is not my favorite, but it's easy to find and is shelf stable. It's starch based, so I don't recommend it for things that you want to stay really moist, such as cake.

rid your baked goods of those pesky eggs. Do keep in mind, though, that very egg-heavy recipes (calling for 3 or more eggs) may need to be slightly reworked in addition to replacing the eggs so they don't get too moist.

THE SKINNY ON FAT

Many of the cakes in this book use oil for their fat. Unless otherwise stated, a mild vegetable oil is the best choice (like canola or a vegetable blend).

The butter that you would normally find in cakes that have a denser crumb or in frosting is easily replaced with a quality margarine. Look for brands like Earth Balance or Spectrum in the health food section of your grocery store. If they aren't available to you, look for margarines that are truly dairy-free (many have whey and other pesky milk byproducts in them). Most margarine has salt in it, which is why most of the cake recipes call for less salt than you may be used to seeing.

Earth Balance and Spectrum also produce some excellent shortenings. If you can't find one of these products, Crisco is vegan. Shortening and margarine are sometimes both called for to make buttercream. While the shortening can be replaced with more margarine, be aware of the shortening's purpose: Margarine doesn't have the same levels of saturated fat, so it doesn't stay as firm at room temperature as shortening does. While margarine can replace shortening, your buttercream may be a little soft.

Some recipes call for the margarine to be at a certain temperature. For room-temperature

margarine, that's exactly what you want: room temperature. Letting it sit out of the refrigerator for about 30 minutes should do the trick. For softened margarine, I usually microwave a stick in 10 second intervals until it's soft enough that it's easily flattened with my finger or a spatula. It should be creamy but not liquefied. Melted margarine should be cooled but liquid, and cold margarine means straight out of the refrigerator.

DON'T GOT MILK

The number of nondairy milks is always on the rise—soy, rice, almond, hemp, hazelnut, oat, coconut (both traditional and suited for drinking)—the list goes on and on. These recipes were tested with a variety of milks and unless one is recommended over another, feel free to use what you prefer. I don't refer to nondairy milks as "milk" because they are milks in their own rights, and I find the quotation marks patronizing.

POUR SOME SUGAR ON ME

Conventional sugar is processed using bone char, and many companies add bleach. Yum. Thankfully, there are plenty of options out there. From organic granulated sugar to evaporated cane juice and less processed sugar like demerara to liquid sweeteners like maple syrup and agave nectar, there are plenty of ways to please your sweet tooth.

When working with a recipe, it's important to note that the kind of sugar used plays a role in the success of the end product. To swap out a solid sweetener, like cane sugar, for a liquid sweetener, like agave nectar, can run the risk of throwing off the whole chemistry of the baked good, in addition to its finished texture. These recipes were formulated using organic granulated sugar. If you are ever curious to check out the processing practices of your local brand of sugar, give them a call or drop them a line. Most companies now are familiar with veganism and will promptly respond to questions you have about their processes and additives.

THE LAND OF CHOCOLATE

One of the most common questions I get is, "Chocolate isn't vegan, is it?" Such silliness . . . We truly can have our cake and vegan, too. And that includes chocolate.

There are some brands that make exclusively vegan chocolate, like Tropical Source. Whole Foods offers store-brand chocolate chips that are labeled vegan, as well. There are more brands out there because most good-quality semisweet chocolate has no dairy in it. The darker the chocolate, the farther away from milk byproducts you get, but always be sure to read the labels.

If you have questions about the origins of the sugar in your chocolate, contact the producer's customer service department for information.

FLOUR POWER

ALL-PURPOSE FLOUR Also known as white flour, this is called for in the majority of recipes in this book. To minimize what we're putting into our bodies, I always recommend buying unbleached flour. The color difference between unbleached and bleached is negligible, and who wants to eat bleach? Yucky.

There are two other types of flour sometimes used in cake baking that you may be familiar with that are **not** used this book. Here's why:

CAKE FLOUR This is white flour that has been processed to have a lower gluten content to make a more delicate crumb. The reason why you won't see it called for in this book is twofold. First, vegan baking doesn't have eggs in it, and eggs typically provide protein (which is what gluten is) and structure (which is what gluten provides). By using all-purpose flour, we increase our gluten content a bit, which helps out our end results. Second, cake flour has less gluten than all-purpose because it's chlorinated. Again, with the chemical baked goods, just say no.

SELF-RISING FLOUR Some cookbooks call for this white flour that has baking powder and salt added. It's hard to find unbleached self-rising flour, and in addition, there's no way of knowing how fresh the flour is and therefore how fresh the baking powder is. We don't want our cakes depending on questionable baking powder. Also, the baking powder used in most self-rising flour is double-acting, which means that it reacts initially when the liquid and dry ingredients make contact and again when exposed to the heat of the oven. It does this with the addition of aluminum, whereas regular baking powder made without aluminum is single-acting. Why do they want to put all of these chemicals in our cakes?!

Long story short, unbleached all-purpose flour is your friend. If you try your hand at some of the gluten-free recipes, you'll have a whole group of new buddies, too.

GLUTEN-FREE BAKING

So, protein in flour (gluten) and protein from eggs traditionally provide baked goods with structure. And we're taking away the gluten and the eggs? Are we crazy? Absolutely not. Vegan, gluten-free baking may seem impossible, but rest assured that thanks to the boundless sea of grains in the world, a tasty gluten-free vegan cake is easy to make and even better to eat.

Gluten-free baking relies on flour blends, as using one flour alone is not entirely possible. The bulk section of your grocery store can often supply these grains, but they are also readily available online. Look for the Bob's Red Mill brand, which not only bakes well but also has very high standards for the quality of production for their gluten-free flours.

BROWN RICE FLOUR This is a very common flour for gluten-free baking. It's light in texture and mild in flavor, exactly what we want in replacing all-purpose flour. It is also easily digestible.

SORGHUM FLOUR Milled from an ancient grain that lends a pleasant mouth feel to gluten-free baked goods, this flour has a very mild flavor.

OAT FLOUR AND OATS These grains can be used in gluten-free baking, but not all oats are created equal, so be sure the oat products you are buying are labeled gluten-free.

TAPIOCA STARCH OR TAPIOCA FLOUR These are actually one and the same. Adding starch to our flour makes it lighter and more cake appropriate.

POTATO STARCH Potato flour is dehydrated potato, essentially instant potatoes, but we want the starch. This is nice and mild and helps make things fluffy.

GUAR GUM AND XANTHAN GUM These are common ingredients you may have noticed when reading labels. They're used as thickeners to help certain products (like nut milks) have a nicer consistency and mouth feel. In baking, they're used in tiny amounts to help replace the binding we would otherwise get from gluten. Guar gum is significantly less expensive than xanthan gum, but some people prefer one over the other. The amounts used are so tiny, that even a spendy bag of gum goes a long way.

OTHER GLUTINOUS SUBSTANCES Some other items to verify gluten-free are your baking powder and vanilla.

CAKE BAKING TIPS FOR TURNING OUT A PERFECT CAKE

FOLLOW THE DIRECTIONS Seems like a no-brainer, but it's easy to assume you know the next step in a recipe, and nothing is worse than realizing, too late, that you guessed wrong. Be sure to read through the whole recipe before starting out.

MIND THE TIME The first time through a recipe, check your cake 5 minutes before you think it's supposed to be done. Variations in altitude and oven temperature, as well as the kind of pan, can affect the speed at which your cake bakes. This will help you learn the nuances of your unique kitchen set up.

AFTER CARE Just because it's out of the oven doesn't mean it's done baking. Some cakes need to cool in the pan, and some cakes need to be inverted soon after exiting the oven so they don't dry out. Again, make sure to read through the directions.

LEAVENING Baking powder and baking soda are our friends, but they can be fickle. If you don't remember when you purchased your current containers of baking powder and baking soda, it's time for new ones. My general rule of thumb is every 6 months.

Baking soda: More than just a freshener for your fridge, baking soda is a natural chemical that acts as a leavener when an acid is added to activate it. Once activated, it creates little air bubbles, which make our cakes nice and fluffy. Some examples of acids are vinegar, lemon juice, or cocoa powder.

Baking powder: Baking powder actually contains baking soda and cream of tartar, which acts as a built-in acid. It also has anti-caking agents, like cornstarch, to keep it from clumping. Baking powder creates a more mild reaction than a strong acid, like vinegar, does, and so sometimes an additional acid is used to help boost the leavening power of the cake batter. If you're out of baking powder, you can always use 1 part baking soda to 2 parts cream of tartar to replace. Also, be sure to look for aluminum-free baking powder. Avoid anything labeled double-acting, as it contains aluminum, and we just don't need that silliness.

THE TROUBLE WITH CAKES ...

While it may be rare, sometimes, despite all your best intentions,
a cake doesn't turn out. Here's how to troubleshoot:

THE PROBLEM	THE POSSIBLE CULPRIT
Sunken center	• Too much liquid • Oven temperature too low • Leavening expired • Underbaking • Opening oven while baking (temperature fluctuations)
Too dense	• Batter not mixed well enough • Too much liquid • Not enough leavening
Cracked top or domed center	• Too much leavening • Too much flour • Oven too hot
Chewy texture	• Overmixing • Not enough sugar
Sticking to pan	• Pan not properly greased and/or floured • Not baked long enough
Sugar "blooming" on cake (looks like little white specks on top of the cake after it cools)	• Sugar not well-blended enough with the margarine or oil before adding dry ingredients

CAKE COSMETIC SURGERY: GOING AU NATUREL

You can't turn on your television without falling upon another cake decorating show. From fancy bakeries to meltdown-triggering competitions, cake decorating is an art form and sport unto itself. Yet, while the cakes are stunning, one thing that never comes up on these shows is the most important factor in the world of cakes: taste.

Think about the things people say about their favorite cake. "This cake is so moist!" or, "This frosting is so creamy!" No one says, "I love how chalky this rolled fondant tastes!" The competitive cake-baking craze has created an unrealistic idea that every cake, in order to be pretty, must be covered in smooth fondant. And while it does make a beautiful cake, no one craves eating it.

Below I have some tips to help you achieve smooth buttercream for cakes you want to appear more refined, as well as some helpful hints for simple, but pretty, cake decoration. I come from the school of thought that says if it's not tasty, it doesn't belong.

CAKE DECORATING

It doesn't require much to build a nice, small arsenal of cake decorating supplies. With just a couple of choice items, you'll have everything you need to make your cake look as great as it tastes.

OFFSET SPATULA This spatula, which looks more like a butter knife on steroids than a spatula, is how bakers get uniform, smooth frosting on the top and sides of a cake. It takes only a little practice before you'll be smoothing with the best of them. Use it in long, slow strokes with even pressure. Also, be sure to read about the crumb coat (page 14) if you have problems with crumbs in your frosting.

FROSTING BAG AND TIPS You might see fancy frosting bag sets with a million tips, and while they're fun, you can get by just fine with a couple of choice tips. Make a throw-away batch of buttercream frosting to play with and pipe away on a sheet of cardboard. It takes only a couple of rounds of practice to perfect some select shapes and designs that will make your cakes all the more lovely.

CAKE LEVELER This device, which looks like a bow for the kitchen, has a metal base with a thin, metal string with an adjustable height. This is a choice tool if you need to trim a little cake off the top to flatten it for stacking layers or to split a thick cake into layers. While a knife works just fine (and if you want to feel like a major badass, look up splitting cakes with dental floss online), a cake leveler ensures that you will get your cakes nice and level and split them evenly.

TEMPERATURE This is the biggest tip for expert cake decorating. It's hard to resist when you know a slice of deliciousness awaits, but icing a warm cake leads to disaster (icing puddle), and trying to cream margarine or shortening that is too hard makes for serious lumps. Slow and steady wins the cake race.

HOW TO FROST A CAKE IN THREE SIMPLE STEPS

1. Let the cake cool completely. This is imperative, or your frosting will melt!

2. Do a crumb coat. This means to apply a superthin layer of frosting to trap in all of the crumbs so they don't lift off and litter your frosting on the surface of the cake. This can be done with your offset spatula, by applying an ultrathin coating (you can usually still see the cake through it). After applying it, place the cake in the refrigerator for 20 to 30 minutes to let it firm up. Skipping this step defeats the purpose of the crumb coat.

3. Slather on the bulk of your frosting. Use an offset spatula to get it smooth. If your frosting is having problems spreading, it may need a splash of whatever milk you are using. If you have leftover frosting, scoop it into an icing bag and fancy up your cake with some piping!

HOW TO FROST MULTILAYER CAKES

Don't let layers intimidate you! It's really easy, I promise.

Begin by placing the bottom layer on a serving platter or cake plate. Then tear small pieces of waxed paper and arrange them around the bottom of the cake, effectively make a cake bib to catch any excess frosting or filling so the plate doesn't get messy.

From there, assess whether the bottom layer is flat on top. If it has a bump, you need to level it, which can be easily done with a knife or a cake leveler (inexpensive ones cost around $5). You can also level it Mafia-style with a piece of dental floss, looping it around the cake bump and pulling it toward you to slice the bump off. The best part of this process is that it makes cake scraps, so you don't have to wait until after dinner to get a taste. If it doesn't look pretty, that's okay because it will be covered up.

Add a large smear of filling or icing on top of the bottom layer up to 1/4 inch from the edge. You'll want the filling to be a little thicker in the center so when the weight of the top layer presses down on it you'll have a nice, solid layer of filling. Now, carefully center the top layer on the cake.

To frost the exterior, begin with the sides and use your offset spatula to smooth the frosting on. From there, coat the top of the cake and decorate as desired. Carefully remove the waxed paper from around the edges, and you're ready to rock!

FROSTING, ICING, AND GLAZE: THE DEBATE THAT COULD END IN A CAKE DOOMSDAY

Most people tend to call the creamy, sugary stuff on top of a cake either frosting or icing. And, like the soda vs. pop debate, this can lead to bar brawls and fighting. But we're making cake here; there shall be no feuds! While you may not distinguish between them, for the sake of this book, I do. To give you a better idea of what to expect, here are my definitions:

FROSTING   This is the fluffy, creamy stuff that you spread in copious amounts and induces sugary, fatty comas of delight.

ICING   This is thinner than frosting, but still has structure. It's high in sugar and low in fat and is usually spread or piped.

GLAZE   Sugar-based and thin, glaze is usually drizzled, poured, or dipped. Think of a glazed donut—it's like a sugar shell. Mmm . . . sugar shell.

WORK IT, CAKE!

Sometimes when I'm decorating a cake, I like to speak in a really exaggerated French accent and pretend I'm a fashion designer. Food is the new high art, right? It doesn't take much effort to make your cake look amazing, and unlike fashion models, we get to have our cake and eat it too! Here are some easy tips to take your cake from looking so-so to catwalk ready in no time:

SPRINKLES   Not just for kids and cupcakes, sprinkles can add that extra somethin' somethin' to a simple cake. Try a contrasting color and experiment with a light sampling of sprinkles or more concentrated and focused applications, like stripes or shapes. You can get the same effect from using coarse, chunky sugar.

POWDERED SUGAR   A light dusting of powdered sugar never hurt any cake, can add a pretty contrast, and is especially nice on cakes with no topping. Be sure to use a fine-mesh sieve to lightly dust the cake. You can play with allover dusting or make a stencil using some waxed paper to sift on a sugar heart or polka dots.

DRIZZLE   Even when you frost a cake, sometimes it needs something else. An accessory, if you will. One of my favorite simple decorations is a small batch of Chocolate Ganache (page 133). Let it drip down the sides of the cake, pipe it on in zigzag stripes, write "Happy Birthday," or add a solid application of a thin, chocolate topping for some extra tastiness. Basic Glaze (page 130) can also add a nice touch. No fancy equipment is needed: Just spoon the glaze into a sandwich bag and snip off the tiniest bit of the corner. Voilà, you're good to go!

GARNISHMENTS   Never underestimate the power of garnish. Putting blueberries in your cake? Reserve some to put on top once it's frosted. A sprinkle of chopped nuts or chocolate-covered espresso beans can add a decorative flair and foreshadow the deliciousness that awaits. Add some fruit sauce or compote when serving. A drizzle of chocolate syrup on the bottom of a plate is a nice touch or some chocolate shavings on top of a cake can quickly take it up a notch. It doesn't need to be flashy or over-the-top. It's just those little finishing touches that make a cake go from nice to wow!

● ● ● CHAPTER 1

Basic Cakes

The basics are a good starting ground. Everyone needs reliable recipes they can turn to for vanilla cake and chocolate cake. Here, you have a traditional option and also a gluten-free version. These cakes can be dressed up with classic vanilla buttercream or chocolate buttercream frosting (pages 139 and 140) or any other number of toppings. The only limit is your imagination!

BASIC VANILLA CAKE

**This is a basic yellow cake recipe, perfect to have under
your belt for birthdays, anniversaries, baby showers, Fridays ...**

INGREDIENTS

3 cups
all-purpose flour

1¹/2 teaspoons
baking powder

1/4 teaspoon
salt

1/2 cup
canola or other mild vegetable oil

2 cups
organic granulated sugar

2 tablespoons
unsweetened applesauce

1¹/2 cups plus 1 tablespoon
nondairy milk

1/2 teaspoon
mild vinegar

2 teaspoons
vanilla extract

DIRECTIONS

Preheat the oven to 350°F. Grease and flour 2 (8-inch) round pans or 1 (9 x 13-inch) pan. Line with parchment paper, if using.

In a small bowl, combine the flour, baking powder, and salt. In a large bowl, preferably with an electric mixer, cream together the oil and sugar until combined. Add the applesauce, milk, vinegar, and vanilla and beat until combined. Let sit for a few minutes to activate the vinegar. Incorporate half the dry ingredients into the wet ingredients, blending until just mixed, then repeat with the other half. Divide the batter between the prepared pans and spread evenly.

Bake for 25 to 30 minutes for 2 round cakes, 37 to 42 minutes for a sheet cake, until a toothpick inserted into the center comes out clean. Let cool in the pan on cooling racks for 15 minutes. Run a butter knife around the edge of the pan and invert onto another cooling rack. Let cool completely before decorating. Store covered at room temperature.

DIFFICULTY:

SERVINGS: 12

BASIC CHOCOLATE CAKE

This chocolate cake is my go-to recipe. It yields the fluffiest, moistest chocolate cake you could ever wish for and works well with a variety of toppings and fillings.

INGREDIENTS

1³/4 cups
all-purpose flour

1¹/2 cups
organic granulated sugar

3/4 cup
baking cocoa, sifted

1¹/2 teaspoons
baking soda

1¹/2 teaspoons
baking powder

1/8 teaspoon
salt

1¹/2 cups
nondairy milk

1/2 teaspoon
mild vinegar

1/2 cup
canola or other mild vegetable oil

2 teaspoons
vanilla extract

1 cup
boiling water

DIRECTIONS

Preheat the oven to 350°F. Lightly grease and flour 2 (8-inch) round pans or 1 (9 x 13-inch) pan. Line with parchment paper, if using.

In a medium bowl, combine the flour, sugar, cocoa, baking soda, baking powder, and salt. In a large bowl, preferably with an electric mixer, combine the milk and vinegar and let sit for a minute to activate the vinegar. Add the oil and vanilla and beat until combined. Incorporate half the dry ingredients into the wet ingredients, blending until just mixed, then repeat with the other half. Add the boiling water and mix to combine. The batter will look very thin. Divide the batter between the prepared pans and spread evenly.

Bake for 28 to 32 minutes for 2 round cakes, 38 to 42 minutes for a sheet cake, until a toothpick inserted into the center comes out clean. Let cool in the pans on cooling racks for 15 minutes. Run a butter knife around the edge of the pan and invert onto another cooling rack. Let cool completely before decorating. Store covered at room temperature.

DIFFICULTY:

SERVINGS: 12

··· have your cake and vegan too ···

GLUTEN-FREE BASIC VANILLA CAKE

Gluten-free doesn't have to mean cake-free! This versatile vanilla
cake is just what you need when you can't have gluten but must have cake.

INGREDIENTS

1 1/2 cups
brown rice flour

1/2 cup
tapioca starch

1/4 cup
potato starch

1 1/4 cups
organic granulated sugar

1 teaspoon
baking powder

1/2 teaspoon
baking soda

1 teaspoon
xanthan gum

1/4 teaspoon
salt

1/4 cup
unsweetened applesauce

1/4 cup
canola or other mild vegetable oil

1 1/4 cups
nondairy milk

1/4 teaspoon
mild vinegar

1 tablespoon
vanilla extract

DIRECTIONS

Preheat the oven to 350°F. This recipe makes 2 thin layers or one thick layer cake, so grease and flour 1 or 2 (8-inch) round pans. Line with parchment paper, if using.

In a small bowl, combine the brown rice flour, tapioca starch, potato starch, sugar, baking powder, baking soda, xanthan gum, and salt. Whisk to combine. In a large bowl, combine the applesauce and oil. Add the milk and vinegar and beat until combined, then let sit for a few minutes to activate the vinegar. Add the vanilla and beat until combined. Incorporate half the dry ingredients into the wet ingredients, blending until just combined, then repeat with the other half. Divide the batter between the prepared pans and spread evenly.

Bake for 22 to 25 minutes for a double-layer cake, 35 to 40 minutes for a single layer, until a toothpick inserted into the center comes out clean. Let the cake(s) cool completely in the pan on a cooling rack. Run a butter knife around the edge of the pan and invert onto another cooling rack. Let cool completely before decorating. Store covered at room temperature.

DIFFICULTY:

SERVINGS: 12

GLUTEN-FREE BASIC CHOCOLATE CAKE

This recipe makes one 9 x 13-inch sheet cake or 2 (8-inch) round cakes, perfect for a birthday cake. Even a discerning palate will be enamored with this moist, chocolaty cake.

INGREDIENTS

1 cup
sorghum flour

1 cup
brown rice flour

1/2 cup
tapioca flour

1/4 cup
potato starch

1 1/2 cups
organic granulated sugar

2/3 cup
baking cocoa, sifted

1 teaspoon
xanthan gum

2 teaspoons
baking powder

1 teaspoon
baking soda

1/4 teaspoon
salt

2 1/2 cups
nondairy milk

1/2 teaspoon
mild vinegar

1/3 cup
canola or other mild vegetable oil

2 teaspoons
vanilla extract

1/2 cup
chocolate chips (optional)

DIRECTIONS

🍫 Preheat the oven to 350°F. Grease and flour 2 (8-inch) round pans or 1 (9 x 13-inch) pan. Line with parchment paper, if using.

🍫 In a medium bowl, combine the sorghum flour, brown rice flour, tapioca flour, potato starch, sugar, cocoa, xanthan gum, baking powder, baking soda, and salt. In a large bowl, preferably with an electric mixer, combine the milk and vinegar and let sit for a few minutes to activate the vinegar. Add the oil and vanilla and beat until combined. Incorporate half the dry ingredients into the wet ingredients, blending until just mixed, then repeat with the other half. Add chocolate chips, if using, and mix just until distributed. Divide the batter between the prepared pans and spread evenly.

🍫 Bake for 25 to 28 minutes for 2 round cakes, 33 to 38 minutes for a sheet cake, until a toothpick inserted into the center comes out clean. Let cool completely in the pan on a cooling rack before decorating. Run a butter knife around the edge of the pan and invert onto another cooling rack. Store covered at room temperature.

DIFFICULTY:

SERVINGS: 12

CHAPTER 2

Breakfast and Snack Cakes

Nothin' says lovin' like cake for breakfast. From simple and mature coffee cakes to more indulgent Bundt cakes, you are sure to find something to satisfy your morning sweet tooth or to curb your appetite throughout the day when you want a little something, but nothing too crazy.

CHERRY OAT SNACK CAKE

This recipe takes a delicious summer staple and turns it into an elegant little cake that will please big and little kids alike. The oatmeal adds a bit of chewy texture, and the mixture of liquid and solid sweetener gives the top of the cake a light crunch in contrast to the sticky sweet cherry bottom.

INGREDIENTS

3 to 4 cups (about 1 pound)
sweet cherries,
pitted and chopped

2/3 cup plus 1 tablespoon
organic granulated sugar

1 1/2 cups
all-purpose flour

1/2 cup
quick-cooking or
old-fashioned oats

1 teaspoon
baking powder

1/2 teaspoon
baking soda

1/4 teaspoon
salt

1/4 cup
margarine, melted

3 tablespoons
agave nectar

2/3 cup
nondairy milk

1/4 teaspoon
mild vinegar

1/2 teaspoon
vanilla extract

powdered sugar for dusting

DIRECTIONS

🐖 Preheat the oven to 350°F. Lightly grease and flour an 8-inch round or square pan.

🐖 Toss the cherries in the 1 tablespoon sugar and scatter evenly in the bottom of the prepared pan. In a small bowl, combine the flour, oats, baking powder, baking soda, and salt. In a medium bowl, preferably with an electric mixer, cream together the remaining 2/3 cup sugar and the margarine until combined. Add the agave, milk, vinegar, and vanilla and mix well. Let sit for a few minutes to activate the vinegar. Incorporate half the dry ingredients into the wet ingredients, blending until just mixed, then repeat with the other half. Carefully spread the batter over the cherries.

🐖 Bake for 35 to 40 minutes, until the cake is browned and a toothpick inserted into the center comes out clean. Let the cake cool completely in the pan on a cooling rack. This cake is served directly out of the pan, because of the cherry bottom. Dust with powdered sugar. Store covered at room temperature.

DIFFICULTY:

SERVINGS: 9

NUTTY 'NANA SNACK CAKE

This cake takes peanut butter and bananas and marries them in an amazing treat that is not only a delicious midday snack but is also just nutritious enough to make you feel like you're healthy for eating it. Almost.

INGREDIENTS

1³/₄ cups
all-purpose flour

1/4 cup
firmly packed brown sugar

1/4 cup
organic granulated sugar

1 teaspoon
baking powder

1/2 teaspoon
baking soda

1/2 teaspoon
ground cinnamon

1/8 teaspoon
salt

1/2 cup
melted margarine,
at room temperature

2/3 cup
natural peanut butter

1/3 cup
nondairy milk

1 large
ripe banana, mashed

coarse sugar for sprinkling

DIRECTIONS

🥄 Preheat the oven to 350°F. Lightly grease an 8-inch square pan or line with parchment paper.

🥄 In a medium bowl, combine the flour, brown sugar, granulated sugar, baking powder, baking soda, cinnamon, and salt. Add the margarine and mix until crumbly. To make the topping, transfer 3/4 cup of the mixture to another bowl, add the peanut butter, mix to combine, and set aside. In another bowl, whisk together the milk and banana. Add the wet ingredients to the original flour mixture and mix to combine. Spread the banana batter evenly into the prepared pan. Crumble the reserved peanut butter topping over the batter and sprinkle with coarse sugar.

🥄 Bake for 32 to 37 minutes, until a toothpick inserted into the center comes out clean. Let the cake cool completely in the pan on a cooling rack. This cake is served from the pan. Store at room temperature, loosely covered.

DIFFICULTY:

SERVINGS: 9

MY-OH-MEYER LEMON BUNDT CAKE

If you can't find Meyer lemons, substitute a mixture of lemon and tangerine zest and juice, but when Meyers are in season, they're a must-have. Tangy and delicious, this cake will perk up the drizzliest winter day.

INGREDIENTS

2 cups
all-purpose flour

1 1/4 cups
coarsely ground quick-cooking or old-fashioned oats

1 1/4 cups
organic granulated sugar

1 tablespoon
baking powder

1/2 teaspoon
baking soda

1/4 teaspoon
salt

1 1/2 cups
nondairy milk

about 3 Meyer lemons
zested and juiced (about 1/3 cup juice)

1/3 cup
canola or other mild vegetable oil

1/2 teaspoon
vanilla extract

1 cup
fresh or frozen berries, such as blueberries or raspberries

powdered sugar for dusting

DIRECTIONS

🐾 Preheat the oven to 350°F. Lightly grease and flour a 15-cup Bundt or other large tube pan.

🐾 In a medium bowl, combine the flour, ground oats, sugar, baking powder, baking soda, and salt. In a large bowl, combine the milk and lemon zest and juice and let sit for a few minutes to activate the citrus. Add the oil and vanilla and mix to combine. Incorporate half the dry ingredients into the wet ingredients, blending until just mixed, then repeat with the other half. Add the berries and gently fold in to avoid streaking. Spread the batter evenly into the prepared pan.

🐾 Bake for 48 to 52 minutes, until a toothpick inserted into the center comes out clean. Let cool in the pan on a cooling rack for 20 minutes. Run a butter knife around the edge of the pan and invert onto another cooling rack, then cool completely. Serve with a light dusting of powdered sugar. Store loosely covered at room temperature.

DIFFICULTY:

SERVINGS: 12

THE GREAT PUMPKIN BUNDT CAKE

This cake has all of the great things of autumn: pumpkin, spices, and a light glaze all wrapped up into a treat that pairs beautifully with tea or coffee, making you feel like you're in some picturesque warm beverage commercial . . . except they don't let you lick the plate clean on TV.

INGREDIENTS

3 cups
all-purpose flour

1 cup
organic granulated sugar

1 tablespoon
baking powder

2 teaspoons
pumpkin pie spice

1 teaspoon
ground cinnamon

1/4 teaspoon
salt

1 cup
pumpkin puree
(not pumpkin pie filling)

1 3/4 cups
nondairy milk

1/2 cup
canola or other mild vegetable oil

2 tablespoons
molasses

1 teaspoon
vanilla extract

1 recipe
Cinnamon Glaze (page 130)

1/2 cup
walnuts or pecans, coarsely
chopped (optional)

powdered sugar for dusting

DIRECTIONS

Preheat the oven to 350°F. Lightly grease a 15-cup Bundt or tube pan.

In a medium bowl, combine the flour, sugar, baking powder, pumpkin pie spice, cinnamon, and salt. In a large bowl, whisk together the pumpkin, milk, oil, molasses, and vanilla. Incorporate half the dry ingredients into the wet ingredients, blending until just mixed, then repeat with the other half. Spread the batter evenly into the prepared pan.

Bake for 42 to 47 minutes, until a toothpick inserted into the center comes out clean. Let cool in the pan on a cooling rack for about 5 minutes. Run a butter knife around the edge of the pan and invert onto another cooling rack. Drizzle the glaze over the warm cake and top with the nuts, if using. After completely cooled, finish the cake with a light dusting of powdered sugar. Store loosely covered at room temperature.

DIFFICULTY:

SERVINGS: 12

SNAZZY, RAZZY ALMOND COFFEE CAKE

Simple yet fancy looking, this coffee cake has a unique texture
due to the helping hand of almond meal. It's delicious and pretty, and sure
to make you the king of the office, should you choose to share.

INGREDIENTS

1 1/3 cups
almond meal

1 2/3 cups
all-purpose flour

2/3 cup
organic granulated sugar

2 teaspoons
baking powder

1/4 teaspoon
salt

1 medium
lemon, zested and juiced
(about 2 tablespoons juice)

1 1/4 cups
nondairy milk

3 tablespoons
canola or other mild vegetable oil

1/2 teaspoon
almond extract (optional)

1 cup raspberries
(fresh, or mostly thawed if frozen)

2 tablespoons
coarse raw sugar

3 tablespoons
slivered almonds

DIRECTIONS

Preheat the oven to 350°F. Lightly grease an 8-inch square pan.

In a small bowl, combine the almond meal, flour, sugar, baking powder, and salt and mix well. In a large bowl, combine the lemon zest and juice and milk. Let sit for a minute to activate the citrus. Add the oil and almond extract, if using. Incorporate half the dry ingredients into the wet ingredients, blending until just mixed, then repeat with the other half. Carefully fold in the raspberries. Spread the batter evenly into the prepared pan. Sprinkle the coarse sugar and almonds over the top.

Bake for 42 to 47 minutes, until golden and a toothpick inserted into the center comes out clean. This cake is served from the pan. Store loosely covered at room temperature.

DIFFICULTY:

SERVINGS: 9

CHOCOLATE CRUMB CAKE

This moist, dense cake is chocolaty and delicious, with a topping that adds crunch. Perfect with a light dusting of powdered sugar and a cup of joe. For an added treat, add 1/3 cup chopped dried cherries to the cake batter.

INGREDIENTS

CRUNCHY CHOCOLATE TOPPING

1 cup plus 2 tablespoons
all-purpose flour

2/3 cup
organic granulated sugar

1/4 cup
baking cocoa, sifted

a pinch
salt

1/2 cup
margarine, melted

1/3 cup
chocolate chips

CAKE

1 1/4 cups
all-purpose flour

1/3 cup
baking cocoa, sifted

1 teaspoon
baking powder

1/2 teaspoon
baking soda

1/4 teaspoon
salt

1/3 cup
canola or other mild vegetable oil

1/2 cup
organic granulated sugar

3/4 cup
nondairy milk

1 teaspoon
vanilla extract

DIRECTIONS

- Preheat the oven to 350°F. Lightly grease a 9-inch springform pan and dust with cocoa.

- To make the topping, in a medium bowl, combine the flour, sugar, cocoa, and salt. Drizzle the margarine over the top and mix with a fork until the mixture is lumpy and the margarine is well incorporated. You may need to use your hands. Add the chocolate chips and mix, then set aside.

- To make the cake, in a small bowl, combine the flour, cocoa, baking powder, baking soda, and salt. In a large bowl, preferably with an electric mixer, cream together the oil and sugar until well combined. Add the milk and vanilla and mix well. Incorporate half the dry ingredients into the wet ingredients, mixing until the batter just comes together, then repeat with the other half. Pour the batter into the prepared pan and spread evenly. Crumble the topping over the batter.

- Bake for 32 to 36 minutes, until a toothpick inserted into the center comes out clean. Let cool completely in the pan on a cooling rack. Run a butter knife around the edge of the pan and release the sides of the springform pan. Store leftover cake loosely covered at room temperature.

DIFFICULTY:

SERVINGS: 12

TIE AN APPLE RIBBON 'ROUND MY COFFEE CAKE

This looks like your typical coffee cake. Beige. Square. Cakey.
But underneath that exterior lies a highly addictive substance, so consider yourself
warned. Thin ribbons of apple create a toothsome texture against the cinnamon
topping. Breakfast nom nom nom.

INGREDIENTS

CAKE

2 medium
apples

2 cups
all-purpose flour

3/4 cup
quick-cooking or old-fashioned
oats, coarsely ground

1 teaspoon
ground cinnamon

1 teaspoon
baking powder

1/2 teaspoon
baking soda

1/4 teaspoon
salt

1/2 cup
margarine, at room temperature

1 cup
organic granulated sugar

1/2 cup
unsweetened applesauce

1 cup
nondairy milk

1 teaspoon
vanilla extract

CINNAMON TOPPING

3/4 cup
organic granulated sugar

1/3 cup
all-purpose flour

1 tablespoon
ground cinnamon

1/4 cup
cold margarine

DIRECTIONS

Preheat the oven to 350°F. Lightly grease and flour a 9 x 13-inch pan.

To make the cake, peel and thinly slice the apples into strips; this is most easily done by cutting the apples into sections with an apple cutter and then thinly slicing the sections. Set aside. In a small bowl, combine the flour, oats, cinnamon, baking powder, baking soda, and salt. In a large bowl, preferably with an electric mixer, cream together the margarine and sugar until combined. Add the applesauce, milk, and vanilla and whisk until smooth. Incorporate half the dry ingredients into the wet ingredients, blending until just mixed, then repeat with the other half. Carefully fold in the apple slices and spread the batter evenly in the pan.

To make the topping, in a small bowl, combine the sugar, flour, and cinnamon. With the back of a fork, mix in the margarine until the mixture is crumbly. Sprinkle the topping over the cake.

Bake for 40 to 45 minutes, until a toothpick inserted into the center comes out clean. Let cool completely in the pan on a cooling rack. This cake is served from the pan. Store cake loosely covered at room temperature.

DIFFICULTY:

SERVINGS: 12

INTENSELY CHOCOLATE BUNDT CAKE

**This cake is not for the faint of heart: Chocolate cake.
Chocolate chips. Chocolate syrup. It's a moist, fudgy Bundt cake
that any serious cacao lover will appreciate.**

INGREDIENTS

CAKE

2¼ cups
all-purpose flour

1/2 cup
baking cocoa, sifted

1½ cups
organic granulated sugar

1 teaspoon
baking powder

1/2 teaspoon
baking soda

1/4 teaspoon
salt

1½ cups
nondairy milk

1/2 cup
canola or other mild vegetable oil

1 teaspoon
vanilla extract

1/2 cup
chocolate chips, coarsely chopped

1/2 cup
chopped walnuts
or pecans (optional)

CHOCOLATE SYRUP

1/4 cup
baking cocoa, sifted

1/2 cup
organic granulated sugar

1/2 cup
water

1/2 teaspoon
vanilla extract

DIRECTIONS

🥄 Preheat the oven to 350°F. Grease and flour well a 15-cup Bundt pan.

🥄 To make the cake, in a medium bowl, combine the flour, cocoa, sugar, baking powder, baking soda, and salt. In a large bowl, preferably with an electric mixer, combine the milk, oil, and vanilla. Incorporate half the dry ingredients into the wet ingredients, blending until just mixed, then repeat with the other half. Gently fold in the chocolate chips and the nuts, if using. Spread the batter evenly into the prepared pan.

🥄 Bake for 38 to 43 minutes, until a toothpick inserted into the center comes out clean. Let cool in the pan on a cooling rack for 20 minutes.

🥄 To make the syrup, combine the cocoa and sugar in a saucepan until there are no more lumps. Whisk in the water and vanilla. Cook on medium heat until the mixture begins to bubble, stirring often. Reduce the heat to low and continue to cook until the sugar dissolves. Remove from the heat and let cool slightly.

🥄 While the cake is still warm, using a butter knife, carefully loosen the edges and center from the pan. Poke holes with a toothpick over the exposed part and carefully pour half of the syrup over the cake. The syrup will take a moment to absorb, then quickly invert the pan onto a platter. Let the cake sit for a minute to help it release before removing the pan. Pour the remaining syrup over the top of the cake. Let the cake cool completely before serving. Store covered at room temperature.

DIFFICULTY LEVEL:

SERVINGS: 12

··· have your cake and vegan too ···

SPICED CRUMB CAKE

Moist cake, crunchy crumb, dense, simple, and delicious: This cake is perfect for those who like a real coffee cake they can enjoy in the morning with little fuss.

INGREDIENTS

CRUNCHY CRUMB TOPPING

1/2 cup
margarine, melted

2/3 cup
firmly packed brown
or other dark sugar

2 teaspoons
ground cinnamon

a pinch
salt

1 1/4 cups
all-purpose flour

CAKE

1 1/2 cups
all-purpose flour

1 teaspoon
baking powder

1/2 teaspoon
baking soda

2 teaspoons
ground cinnamon

1 teaspoon
ground ginger

1/4 teaspoon
ground nutmeg

1/4 teaspoon
ground cardamom

1/4 teaspoon
salt

6 tablespoons
margarine,
at room temperature

1/2 cup
organic granulated sugar

1/4 cup
unsweetened applesauce

2/3 cup
nondairy milk

1 tablespoon
molasses

1 teaspoon
vanilla extract

powdered sugar for dusting

DIRECTIONS

- Preheat the oven to 350°F. Lightly grease and flour a 9-inch springform pan or an 8-inch square pan.

- To make the topping, in a medium bowl, preferably with an electric mixer, cream together the margarine, sugar, cinnamon, and salt until combined. Add the flour, 1/4 cup at a time, until a crumbly mixture comes together that you can easily form with your hands. Set aside.

- To make the cake, in a medium bowl, preferably with an electric mixer, combine the flour, baking powder, baking soda, cinnamon, ginger, nutmeg, cardamom, and salt. In a large bowl, cream together the margarine, sugar, and applesauce until combined. Add the milk, molasses, and vanilla and mix well. Incorporate half the dry ingredients into the wet ingredients, blending until just mixed, then repeat with the other half. Spread the batter evenly into the prepared pan. Crumble the topping over the batter.

- Bake for 35 to 40 minutes, until lightly browned and a toothpick inserted into the center comes out clean. Let the cake cool completely in the pan on a cooling rack. Dust with powdered sugar and store covered at room temperature.

DIFFICULTY:

SERVINGS: 12

PRESSED PLUM COFFEE CAKE

This is a simple cake that really shows off the beautiful colors and vibrant flavors of the plums in a moist, dense cake that's perfect for breakfast.

INGREDIENTS

1 1/2 cups
all-purpose flour

1 teaspoon
baking powder

1/4 teaspoon
salt

1/4 cup
margarine, at room temperature

1/3 cup
firmly packed brown sugar

1/3 cup
nondairy milk

1/4 cup
unsweetened applesauce

1/2 teaspoon
vanilla extract

1 1/2 cups
pitted and quartered plums

2 tablespoons
coarse sugar

DIRECTIONS

Preheat the oven to 375°F. Grease and flour an 8-inch round or square pan. Line the bottom with parchment paper, if using.

In a small bowl, combine the flour, baking powder, and salt. In a medium bowl, preferably with an electric mixer, cream together the margarine and sugar until combined. Add the milk, applesauce, and vanilla and whisk until well combined. Incorporate half the dry ingredients into the wet ingredients, blending until just mixed, then repeat with the other half. Spread the batter evenly into the prepared pan. Toss the plum quarters with 1 tablespoon of the coarse sugar and press the plums into the batter, cut side up. Sprinkle the remaining 1 tablespoon sugar over the batter.

Bake for 32 to 38 minutes, until a toothpick inserted into the center comes out clean. Let the cake cool completely in the pan on a cooling rack. Run a butter knife around the edge of the pan and carefully transfer to a platter. Store covered at room temperature.

DIFFICULTY:

SERVINGS: 10 to 12

CHAPTER 3

Simple Layer Cakes

These single-layer cakes are things of beauty: no fillings, no stacking of layers. Heck, some of them even have their topping built-in—just bake and flip! Simple, sweet, and in your mouth, just the way a cake should be.

BANANA FUDGE STRIPED CAKE

**This is a supersimple sheet cake that's perfectly sweet
by itself, but rocks warm with a scoop of ice cream. Nom!**

INGREDIENTS

FUDGE STRIPE SAUCE

1/3 cup
chocolate chips

1 teaspoon
agave nectar, corn syrup,
or brown rice syrup

1 tablespoon
nondairy milk

2 tablespoons
margarine

CAKE

2 cups
all-purpose flour

1 1/4 cups
organic granulated sugar

2 teaspoons
baking powder

1/2 teaspoon
baking soda

1/4 teaspoon
salt

3/4 cup
nondairy milk

1/2 teaspoon
mild vinegar

1 cup
mashed ripe banana

1/4 cup
canola or other mild vegetable oil

1 teaspoon
vanilla extract

1 large
ripe but firm banana,
sliced into thin rounds

DIRECTIONS

- To make the sauce, in a small saucepan, combine the chocolate chips, agave, milk, and margarine. Cook on medium heat, stirring frequently, until the chocolate and margarine melt. Whisk to combine and remove from the heat. Let the mixture cool.

- Preheat the oven to 350°F. Lightly grease and flour an 8-inch square pan.

- To make the cake, in a medium bowl, combine the flour, sugar, baking powder, baking soda, and salt. In a large bowl, combine the milk and vinegar and let sit for a few minutes to activate the vinegar. Add the mashed banana, oil, and vanilla and mix until combined. Incorporate half the dry ingredients into the wet ingredients, blending until just mixed, then repeat with the other half. Fold in the banana slices. Spread the banana mixture evenly into the prepared pan. Drizzle the cooled fudge sauce in stripes along the banana mixture. Run a butter knife through the stripes to make a nice zigzag pattern.

- Bake for 37 to 42 minutes, until a toothpick inserted into the center comes out clean. Let cool in the pan on a cooling rack for 40 to 60 minutes before serving. Store covered in the refrigerator.

DIFFICULTY:

SERVINGS: 9

ZUCCHINI CAKE WITH CINNAMON CREAM CHEESE FROSTING

Oh. My. Goodness. This is such a *perfect* cake for summer. A light, simple, creamy, flavorful, moist zucchini cake with cinnamon cream cheese frosting. Yes, please! You can opt to make this cake as a double-layer cake rather than a single one. There is ample frosting.

INGREDIENTS

1 1/2 cups plus 2 tablespoons all-purpose flour

3/4 cup plus 2 tablespoons organic granulated sugar

1 teaspoon baking powder

1/2 teaspoon baking soda

1/4 teaspoon salt

1 cup nondairy milk

1/4 teaspoon mild vinegar

1/4 cup canola or other mild vegetable oil

1 teaspoon vanilla extract

1 cup packed finely shredded zucchini, drained of excess juice

1 recipe Cinnamon Cream Cheese Frosting (see page 138)

DIRECTIONS

🥄 Preheat the oven to 350°F. Lightly grease and flour the sides of 1 or 2 (8- or 9-inch) round pans and line with parchment paper.

🥄 In a medium bowl, combine the flour, sugar, baking powder, baking soda, and salt. In a large bowl, combine the milk and vinegar and let sit for a few minutes to activate the vinegar. Add the oil and vanilla and mix to combine. Incorporate half the dry ingredients into the wet ingredients, blending until just mixed, then repeat with the other half. Add the zucchini and mix until evenly distributed. Divide the batter between the prepared pans and spread evenly.

🥄 Bake for 22 to 28 minutes for 1 cake, 40 to 45 minutes for 2 cakes, until a toothpick inserted into the center comes out clean and the cake is light and springs back to the touch. Let cool in the pans on a cooling rack for 20 minutes. Run a butter knife around the edge of one of the layers and invert onto the cooling rack. Let cool completely before frosting. Spread the frosting over the top. Remove the other layer from its pan and place on the bottom layer. Spread more frosting over the top and sides. If you are making 1 layer, you will have enough frosting to bust out the piping bag and add some decorative frosting work to the top. You will need to add a little more sugar to the piping frosting to make it a bit stiffer so it holds its shape. (See page 14 for more tips on frosting cakes.) Store covered in the refrigerator.

DIFFICULTY:

SERVINGS: 12

AMY'S HUH WHAT PEACH CAKE

Essentially an upside-down cake, this confection was inspired by my BFF Amy's love of summer fruit and inappropriate taste in music, along with the flavors of the famous Peach Melba. The peach cake is incredibly impressive for minimal effort. It's tender and delicious and becomes intoxicating when paired with the raspberry crème topping.

INGREDIENTS

2 tablespoons
organic granulated sugar

2 tablespoons
cold margarine,
cut into small pieces

3 to 4
ripe but firm peaches, pitted, and
cut into slices 3/4 to 1 inch wide
(about 8 slices per peach)

1 1/2 cups
all-purpose flour

2 teaspoons
baking powder

1/4 teaspoon
salt

1/4 cup
unsweetened applesauce

3/4 cup
firmly packed brown sugar

1/3 cup
canola or other mild vegetable oil

3/4 cup
nondairy milk

1 teaspoon
vanilla extract

1 recipe
Raspberry Crème (page 135)

DIRECTIONS

🐾 Preheat the oven to 350°F. Grease well and flour an 8-inch round pan and line the bottom with parchment paper. If you do not use parchment, be sure to grease the bottom really well or use a springform pan to ensure the peaches will release.

🐾 In the bottom of the prepared baking pan, sprinkle the granulated sugar and scatter the margarine. Arrange the peach slices in a single-layer circle, covering the bottom of the pan. In a small bowl, combine the flour, baking powder, and salt. In a medium bowl, preferably with an electric mixer, cream together the applesauce and brown sugar until combined. Add the oil, milk, and vanilla and mix well. Incorporate half the dry ingredients into the wet ingredients, blending until just mixed, then repeat with the other half. Spread the batter evenly over the peach mixture, being careful not to disturb the peaches. Leave a 3/4-inch margin at the top of the pan.

🐾 Bake for 40 to 45 minutes, until the cake is browned and a toothpick inserted into the center comes out cleanish (because of the peaches, it will not be completely clean). Let cool for 5 minutes in the pan on a cooling rack. Loosen the edges of the cake with a butter knife and invert onto a platter. Let sit for a few moments as the peaches release, then carefully remove the pan. Serve the cake warm with the crème. Store leftover cake covered in the refrigerator.

DIFFICULTY: 🥄🥄🥄

SERVINGS: 12

PAPPY'S PISTACHIO TEA CAKE

My grandfather used to make pistachio pudding when I was a child, and I always eagerly anticipated eating it up, warm from the stovetop. This cake is moist and delicate, while the fragrance of the pistachios makes it subtle yet perfectly decadent.

INGREDIENTS

1 cup
ground pistachios (about 8 ounces shelled pistachios; salted is fine)

1 3/4 cups
all-purpose flour

1 cup
organic granulated sugar

2 teaspoons
baking powder

1/4 teaspoon
salt (1/8 teaspoon if using salted pistachios)

1 (8-ounce) container
soy cream cheese, at room temperature

1 1/3 cups
nondairy milk

1/4 cup
canola or other mild vegetable oil

1 teaspoon
vanilla extract

1 recipe
Chocolate Sauce (page 133)

pistachios for garnish
shelled, chopped or whole

DIRECTIONS

Preheat the oven to 350°F. Grease and flour an 8- or 9-inch pan and/or line the bottom with parchment paper.

In a small bowl, combine the ground pistachios, flour, sugar, baking powder, and salt. In a medium bowl, preferably using an electric mixer, mix the cream cheese and some of the milk until combined. Incorporate half the remaining milk, blending until just mixed, then repeat with the other half. Add the oil and vanilla and mix until combined. Incorporate half the dry ingredients into the wet ingredients, blending until just mixed, then repeat with the other half. Spread evenly into the prepared pan.

Bake for 40 to 45 minutes, until a toothpick inserted into the center comes out mostly clean, but there might be some little crumbs clinging to it. Let cool in the pan on a cooling rack for 15 minutes. Run a butter knife around the edge of the pan and invert onto another cooling rack. Let cool completely. Serve the cake with warm chocolate sauce drizzled on top and some pistachio garnish. Store leftover cake in the refrigerator.

DIFFICULTY:

SERVINGS: 12

TORTA LIMONE

This cake is very grown-up. Subtle, with unusual ingredients and lots of nuance in each bite, it is at once complex yet understated. Be sure to use a finely ground cornmeal so you don't end up with hard bits.

INGREDIENTS

1 1/3 cups
all-purpose flour

1/3 cup
finely ground cornmeal

1 teaspoon
baking powder

1/2 teaspoon
baking soda

1/4 teaspoon
salt

1 cup
organic granulated sugar

1/3 cup
olive oil

1 medium
lemon, zested and juiced (about 2 tablespoons juice)

2/3 cup
nondairy milk

1 recipe
Basic Glaze (page 130)

DIRECTIONS

Preheat the oven to 350°F. Lightly grease and flour an 8-inch round pan or springform pan.

In a small bowl, combine the flour, cornmeal, baking powder, baking soda, and salt. In a medium bowl, combine the sugar and olive oil and mix until well combined. Add the lemon zest and juice and the milk and mix until well combined. Incorporate half the dry ingredients into the wet ingredients, blending until just mixed, then repeat with the other half. Spread the batter evenly into the prepared pan.

Bake for 32 to 37 minutes, until a toothpick inserted into the center comes out clean. Let the cake cool completely in the pan on a cooling rack. Run a butter knife around the edge of the pan and gently transfer onto a platter. Spread the glaze on the cooled cake. Store loosely covered at room temperature.

DIFFICULTY:

SERVINGS: 12

CARDAMOM CASHEW CAKE

Kheer is a traditional Indian rice pudding that incorporates cardamom, cashews, and raisins into heavenly perfection. This cake is inspired by those flavors and is a unique change from more traditional cakes.

INGREDIENTS

1¹/2 cups
all-purpose flour

2 teaspoons
baking powder

1 ¹/2 teaspoons
ground cardamom

¹/2 teaspoon
ground cinnamon

¹/4 teaspoon
salt

¹/4 cup
unsweetened applesauce

1 cup
organic granulated sugar

3/4 cup
nondairy milk

¹/3 cup
canola or other mild vegetable oil

1 teaspoon
vanilla extract

¹/2 cup
golden raisins

¹/3 cup
raw cashew bits

1 recipe
Cashew Icing (page 132)

DIRECTIONS

🍮 Preheat the oven to 350°F. Lightly grease and flour an 8-inch pan. Line the bottom with parchment paper, if using.

🍮 In a medium bowl, combine the flour, baking powder, cardamom, cinnamon, and salt. In a large bowl, using an electric mixer, combine the applesauce and sugar. Add the milk, oil, and vanilla and mix until creamy. Incorporate half the dry ingredients into the wet ingredients, blending until just mixed, then repeat with the other half. Gently mix in the raisins and cashew bits. Spread the batter evenly into the prepared pan.

🍮 Bake for 32 to 36 minutes, until golden and a toothpick inserted into the center comes out clean. Let cool completely in the pan on a cooling rack. Run a butter knife around the edge of the pan and invert onto a platter. Pour the icing over the completely cooled cake and gently spread to coat. Store covered at room temperature.

DIFFICULTY:

SERVINGS: 12

GLUTEN-FREE MEXICAN CHOCOLATE TORTE

This cake is simple, yet so rich and complex in flavor and texture that you'll feel like it took a lot more effort than you did to make it. So put your feet up and enjoy a slice of your hard work! If you're feeling adventurous, add the chipotle pepper. Feeling more conservative? The cinnamon is delicious on its own. Don't need gluten-free? Omit the brown rice flour and use 1/4 cup all-purpose flour.

INGREDIENTS

1 1/4 cups
chocolate chips

1/2 cup
margarine

1/2 (12-ounce) package
firm silken aseptic tofu

1/2 cup
organic granulated sugar

1 1/2 cups
almond meal

1/4 cup
brown rice flour

1 teaspoon
ground cinnamon

1/8 to 1/4 teaspoon
ground chipotle pepper (optional)

1/4 cup
powdered sugar for dusting

DIRECTIONS

🍫 Preheat the oven to 300°F. Lightly grease an 8- or 9-inch springform pan and dust with gluten-free flour.

🍫 In a small saucepan, melt the chocolate and margarine, stirring frequently. Remove from the heat and let cool. In the bowl of a food processor, puree the tofu. Add the chocolate mixture and blend until smooth. Add the sugar, almond meal, flour, cinnamon, and chipotle, if using, and blend until creamy. Spread the mixture evenly into the prepared pan.

🍫 Bake for 50 to 55 minutes, until a toothpick inserted into the center comes out relatively clean. Let the cake cool completely in the pan on a cooling rack. Run a butter knife around the edge of the pan and release the sides of the springform pan. Leave the cake on the springform pan bottom. Dust with powdered sugar. Store covered at room temperature.

DIFFICULTY:

SERVINGS: 12

BANANAS FOSTER CAKE

This elegant, simple cake is best served fresh and warm. While somewhat unusual, its flavor is intoxicating and will quickly win over the biggest skeptics.

INGREDIENTS

1/4 cup
margarine

3 tablespoons
organic granulated sugar

2 tablespoons
rum

2 to 3 large or 3 to 4 medium
ripe but firm bananas

1 1/2 cups
all-purpose flour

3/4 cup
firmly packed brown sugar

1 1/2 teaspoons
baking powder

1/2 teaspoon
baking soda

1/4 teaspoon
salt

1 cup
nondairy milk

1/4 teaspoon
mild vinegar

1/4 cup
canola or other mild vegetable oil

1/2 teaspoon
vanilla extract

1 teaspoon maple extract
(optional, replace with vanilla if not using)

DIRECTIONS

Preheat the oven to 350°F. Grease and flour an 8-inch round pan and line with parchment paper. Parchment is very important for this recipe. Otherwise, you can try using a well-greased springform pan, with the bottom wrapped in tin foil to avoid any dripping, but be warned that the bottom will leave a pattern on your bananas!

In a small saucepan, combine the margarine, granulated sugar, and rum. Heat on medium heat until the margarine is melted and all the ingredients are incorporated. Pour into the prepared pan. Slice the bananas in half lengthwise and then in half crosswise. Arrange the bananas with the rounded side down in the pan, cutting and arranging as needed to fill the bottom of the pan. In a small bowl, combine the flour, brown sugar, baking powder, baking soda, and salt. In a large bowl, combine the milk and vinegar and let sit for a few minutes to activate the vinegar. Add the oil, vanilla, and maple extract, if using, whisking well. Incorporate half the dry ingredients into the wet ingredients, blending until just mixed, then repeat with the other half. Spread the batter evenly into the prepared pan, being mindful to not disturb the bananas. Leave a 3/4-inch margin at the top.

Bake for 32 to 35 minutes, until a toothpick inserted into the center comes out clean. Let cool in the pan on a cooling rack for 5 minutes. Run a butter knife around the edge of the pan and invert onto a platter. Let sit for 5 minutes before removing the pan and carefully peeling back the parchment. This cake is best served the day it's made, as the bananas begin to look a little strange, but you can store it covered in the refrigerator.

DIFFICULTY:

SERVINGS: 8

ANISE ORANGE CAKE

This simple cake features an unusual topping: a mixture of sugar and orange zest. The oil from the zest provides just enough moisture to transform the sugar into a crunchy little topping, contrasting the light, moist anise cake. You can choose to serve this cake by itself or accompany with the orange cranberry compote.

INGREDIENTS

CAKE

1 1/2 cups
all-purpose flour

1 teaspoon
baking powder

3/4 teaspoon
anise seeds, or 1/2 teaspoon ground anise

1/4 teaspoon
salt

1/2 cup
margarine, at room temperature

1 cup
organic granulated sugar

3/4 cup
nondairy milk

1/2 teaspoon
mild vinegar

1/2 teaspoon
vanilla extract

ORANGE CRANBERRY COMPOTE

1 medium
orange, zested and segmented

3/4 cup
chopped cranberries

1/4 cup
agave nectar

1/2 teaspoon
vanilla extract

TOPPING

3 tablespoons
organic granulated sugar

DIRECTIONS

- Preheat the oven to 350°F. Lightly grease and flour an 8-inch round pan and line the bottom with parchment paper, if using.

- To make the cake, in a small bowl, combine the flour, baking powder, anise, and salt. In a large bowl, preferably with an electric mixer, cream together the margarine and sugar until smooth and creamy. Add the milk, vinegar, and vanilla and blend well. Incorporate half the dry ingredients into the wet ingredients, blending until just mixed, then repeat with the other half. Spread the batter evenly into the prepared pan.

- Bake for 32 to 36 minutes, until lightly golden and a toothpick inserted into the center comes out clean. Let cool in the pan on a cooling rack for 20 minutes. Loosen the edges of the cake with a butter knife and invert onto another cooling rack. Let cool completely before decorating.

- While the cake is cooling, make the compote, if using. In a saucepan, combine the orange segments (reserve the orange zest for the topping), cranberries, agave, and vanilla. Cook on medium heat, stirring often, for about 5 minutes, until the cranberries burst and begin to release their juices. Remove from the heat and let cool. Store the compote in the refrigerator.

- When the cake is cool, make the topping. In a small bowl, mix the sugar and reserved orange zest until mealy, with a texture like moist sand. Spread the topping over the cake and let sit for about 20 minutes, until dried and set. If using, bring the compote to room temperature before serving.

DIFFICULTY:

SERVINGS: 12

POTLUCK PINEAPPLE UPSIDE-DOWN CAKE

The addition of the semolina flour gives this cake a delicate crumb, which pairs deliciously with the buttery pineapple. Your grandma would be proud.

INGREDIENTS

1/4 **cup**
margarine

1/4 **cup**
firmly packed brown sugar

3/4 **cup**
semolina flour

3/4 **cup**
all-purpose flour

1/3 **cup**
organic granulated sugar

1 **teaspoon**
baking powder

1/2 **teaspoon**
baking soda

1/4 **teaspoon**
salt

3/4 **cup**
nondairy milk

1/4 **teaspoon**
mild vinegar

3 **tablespoons**
canola or other mild vegetable oil

1 **teaspoon**
vanilla extract

1 **(20-ounce) can**
pineapple rings, drained

maraschino cherries (optional)

DIRECTIONS

Preheat the oven to 350°F. Lightly grease and flour the sides of an 8- or 9-inch round pan. Line the bottom with greased parchment paper. If you don't have parchment, grease the bottom of the pan really well.

In a saucepan, combine the margarine and brown sugar and cook on medium heat, stirring often, until the margarine is melted and the sugar dissolves. Remove from the heat. In a large bowl, combine the semolina flour, all-purpose flour, granulated sugar, baking powder, baking soda, and salt. In a medium bowl, combine the milk and vinegar and let sit for a few minutes to activate the vinegar. Add the oil and vanilla and mix until combined. Incorporate half the dry ingredients into the wet ingredients, blending until just mixed, then repeat with the other half. Scrape the brown sugar mixture into the prepared pan and spread evenly. Arrange the pineapple rings and cherries, if using, on top of the brown sugar mixture in a single layer. Spread the cake batter evenly on top of the pineapple. Leave a 3/4-inch margin at the top of the pan.

Bake for 28 to 35 minutes, until a toothpick inserted into the center comes out clean and the top is golden. Let the cake rest on a cooling rack for 5 minutes. Loosen the edges of the cake with a butter knife and invert onto a platter. Leave the pan on the cake and let it sit, upside-down, for 5 more minutes. Then carefully remove the pan and peel off the parchment. Serve warm or at room temperature. Store leftover cake sealed at room temperature.

DIFFICULTY:

SERVINGS: 8 to 10

SUNNY PUDDIN' POKE CAKE

Essential for potlucks and summer picnics, this cake delivers
a nostalgic taste mixed with a lesser-used flavor combination:
chocolate and lemon. The result is pure magic.

INGREDIENTS

CAKE

1³/4 cups
all-purpose flour

1¹/2 cups
organic granulated sugar

3/4 cup
baking cocoa, sifted

1¹/2 teaspoons
baking powder

1¹/2 teaspoons
baking soda

1/8 teaspoon
salt

1¹/2 cups
nondairy milk

1/2 teaspoon
mild vinegar

1/2 cup
canola or other mild vegetable oil

2 teaspoons
vanilla extract

1 cup
boiling water

LEMON PUDDIN'

1/4 cup
cornstarch

1 cup
organic granulated sugar

2 1/2 cups
nondairy milk

1 medium
lemon, zested

1/4 cup
lemon juice

DIRECTIONS

🥄 Preheat the oven to 350°F. Lightly grease and flour a 9 x 13-inch pan.

🥄 To make the cake, in a medium bowl, combine the flour, sugar, cocoa, baking powder, baking soda, and salt. In a large bowl combine the milk and vinegar and let sit for a minute to react. Add the oil and vanilla and mix until combined. Incorporate half the dry ingredients into the wet ingredients, blending until just mixed, then repeat with the other half. Add the boiling water and mix to combine. The batter will look very thin. Spread the batter evenly into the prepared pan.

🥄 Bake for 37 to 42 minutes, until a toothpick inserted into the center comes out clean. Let the cake cool completely in the pan on a cooling rack.

🥄 While the cake is baking, make the pudding. In a medium saucepan, combine the cornstarch and sugar and mix to break up any lumps. Whisk in the milk and mix well to combine. Cook over medium-high heat for about 10 minutes, whisking constantly, until the mixture begins to bubble. Lower the heat to medium-low and add the lemon zest and juice. Mix well and continue to cook for 5 to 8 minutes, until the mixture begins to thicken and coats the back of a spoon. Remove from the heat.

🥄 With the end of a wooden spoon, poke holes all over the cake. Pour half of the warm pudding mixture over the cake and smooth over to fill the holes. Let the remaining pudding cool to room temperature, stirring occasionally. Spread the remaining pudding over the cake as the topping. Store the cake covered in its pan in the refrigerator. Cut and serve the cake cold from the pan.

DIFFICULTY: 🥄🥄

SERVINGS: 12

CHAPTER 4

Multilayer Cakes

The multilayer cake, bringer of much fear to many a kitchen. Relax!
It's not as scary as it seems. These recipes will prove to you what
a badass baker you truly are as you level, layer, and frost your way
through these cakes.

BIG DEBBIE'S CREAM CAKE

When I was in school, no lunch was complete without a Little Debbie snack of some sort. Now you can enjoy a full-size vegan oatmeal cream cake. Be sure to pair a slice with an oversize glass of soy milk.

INGREDIENTS

CAKE

1 cup plus 1/4 cup
nondairy milk

1 cup
raisins

1/2 cup
margarine, melted

1 tablespoon
molasses

2 teaspoons
vanilla extract

1 1/2 cups
quick-cooking or old-fashioned oats

1 cup
all-purpose flour

1/2 cup
organic granulated sugar

1 teaspoon
baking powder

2 teaspoons
ground cinnamon

1/4 teaspoon
salt

CREAM FILLING

1/4 cup
margarine, at room temperature

1/4 cup
shortening, at room temperature

1/2 teaspoon
vanilla extract

2 cups
powdered sugar, sifted

a splash
nondairy milk

DIRECTIONS

🍳 Preheat the oven to 350°F. Grease and flour 2 (8-inch) round pans and line with parchment paper.

🍳 To make the cake, in a small saucepan, combine 1 cup milk and the raisins. Cook over medium heat until the liquid comes to a simmer. Remove from the heat and let cool. Transfer the mixture to a food processor and pulse until the raisins are pureed into the milk. Add the margarine, molasses, vanilla, and the remaining 1/4 cup milk and process to combine. In a small bowl, combine the oats, flour, sugar, baking powder, cinnamon, and salt. Incorporate half the dry ingredients into the wet ingredients, blending until just mixed, then repeat with the other half. Divide the batter between the prepared pans and spread evenly.

🍳 Bake for 25 to 28 minutes, until a toothpick inserted into the center comes out clean. Let cool in the pans on cooling racks. Cool completely before filling.

🍳 To make the filling, using an electric mixer, cream the margarine and shortening together. Add the vanilla and powdered sugar, and beat well, until fluffy. If the cream is not as smooth as you would like, add the splash of milk.

🍳 To assemble the cake, run a butter knife around the edge of one of the layers and invert onto a platter. This will have the bottom layer upside down, so its top should be flat. Spread the cream evenly on top. Remove the other layer from its pan and place on the bottom layer. Store in a sealed container at room temperature. This cake is actually better made a day ahead so the flavors have time to meld.

DIFFICULTY:

SERVINGS: 12

PEANUT BUTTER CHOCOLATE DREAM CAKE

Decadent, but not too rich, this cake will make the PB and chocolate lovers in your life swoon! This is a favorite recipe in our house. Whoever gets the last piece reigns triumphant but is responsible for baking the cake next time.

INGREDIENTS

CAKE

1 1/2 cups
all-purpose flour

1/4 cup
baking cocoa (preferably Dutch processed), sifted

1 cup
organic granulated sugar

1 teaspoon
baking powder

1/4 teaspoon
salt

1 cup
nondairy milk, at room temperature

1/4 teaspoon
mild vinegar

1/4 cup
chocolate chips, melted and cooled

1/4 cup
canola or other mild vegetable oil

1 teaspoon
vanilla extract

PB FILLING

1/3 cup
natural peanut butter

2 tablespoons
margarine, at room temperature

1 cup
powdered sugar, as needed

1 teaspoon
nondairy milk, if needed

PB GANACHE TOPPING

1 recipe
Chocolate Ganache (page 133)

1 tablespoon
natural peanut butter

DIRECTIONS

- Preheat the oven to 350°F. Grease and flour 2 (8-inch) round pans and line with parchment paper.

- To make the cake, in a small bowl, combine the flour, cocoa, sugar, baking powder, and salt. In a large bowl, combine the milk and vinegar and let sit for a few minutes to activate the vinegar. Add the melted chocolate, oil, and vanilla, whisking well. Incorporate half the dry ingredients into the wet ingredients, blending until just mixed, then repeat with the other half. Divide the batter into the prepared pans and spread evenly.

- Bake for 25 to 28 minutes until a toothpick inserted into the center comes out clean. Let cool in the pans on cooling racks for 15 minutes. Loosen the edges of the cake with a butter knife and invert onto other cooling racks. Let cool completely before frosting.

- To make the filling, in a medium bowl, using an electric mixer, combine the peanut butter and margarine. Add the powdered sugar in batches until the filling is sweetened to your desire. Add the milk, if needed, to make the mixture spreadable.

- Wait until you are almost ready to assemble the cake before making the topping. Prepare the ganache according to the directions, with the addition of the peanut butter.

- To assemble the cake, center the bottom layer on a platter. If needed, level the top of the cake using a cake level or a knife. Spread the peanut butter filling evenly over the top. Place the other layer on top of the frosted bottom. Carefully spread on the ganache and let set for about 30 minutes before serving. (See page 14 for more tips on frosting cakes.) Store in a covered container.

DIFFICULTY:

SERVINGS: 8

ALMOND MOCHA CAKE

This cake has it all: moist cake, creamy chocolate ganache filling, and a velvet coffee buttercream that will delight even the fussiest coffee haters.

INGREDIENTS

1 3/4 cups
all-purpose flour

3/4 cup
almond meal

1 teaspoon
baking powder

1/2 teaspoon
baking soda

1/4 teaspoon
salt

1/2 cup
margarine, at room temperature

1 1/4 cups
organic granulated sugar

1/4 cup
unsweetened applesauce

1 cup
nondairy milk

1/2 teaspoon
almond extract (optional)

1 recipe
Chocolate Ganache (page 133)

1 recipe
Coffee Buttercream (page 141)

coffee beans or chocolate-covered espresso beans for decoration

DIRECTIONS

🍮 Preheat the oven to 350°F. Grease and flour 2 (8-inch) round pans and line with parchment paper. This cake is a bit delicate, so if not using parchment, make sure the pans are very well greased and floured.

🍮 In a small bowl, combine the flour, almond meal, baking powder, baking soda, and salt. In a large bowl, preferably using an electric mixer, cream together the margarine and sugar until smooth. Add the applesauce, milk, and almond extract, if using, and mix until combined. Incorporate half the dry ingredients into the wet ingredients, blending until just mixed, then repeat with the other half. Divide the batter between the prepared pans and spread evenly.

🍮 Bake for 25 to 28 minutes, until a toothpick inserted into the center comes out clean. Let cool completely in the pans on cooling racks.

🍮 To assemble the cake, run a butter knife around the edge of one of the layers and invert onto a platter. Be sure to remove parchment paper from the bottom of the cake, if used. If needed, level the top of the cake using a cake level or a knife. Spread the ganache on top, within 1/4 inch of the edge. Remove the other layer from its pan and place on the bottom layer. Level it if you'd like. Spread the coffee buttercream over the top and sides. (See page 14 for more tips on frosting cakes.) Decorate with coffee beans or chocolate-covered espresso beans. Store covered at room temperature.

DIFFICULTY:

SERVINGS: 8 to 10

CHOCOCONUTTY CREAM CAKE

Here's a cake for people who love the flavor of coconut, but not so much the texture, and chocolate, too, of course! This moist cake is filled with coconut custard and a chocolaty frosting, reminiscent of milk chocolate.

INGREDIENTS

CAKE

2 cups
all-purpose flour

1/2 cup
finely ground coconut
(process the finely shredded
kind in a food processor)

2 teaspoons
baking powder

1/2 teaspoon
baking soda

1/4 teaspoon
salt

1 1/2 cups
organic granulated sugar

1/4 cup
unsweetened applesauce

1/4 cup
canola or other mild vegetable oil

1 teaspoon
vanilla extract

1/2 cup
coconut milk

1/2 cup
other nondairy milk

COCONUT CUSTARD

1/4 cup
organic granulated sugar

2 tablespoons
cornstarch

1 cup
coconut milk

1 recipe
Chocolate Buttercream (page 140)

flaked coconut for garnish
(optional)

DIRECTIONS

🍮 Preheat the oven to 350°F. Lightly grease and flour 2 (8-inch) round pans and line with parchment paper.

🍮 To make the cake, in a small bowl, combine the flour, ground coconut, baking powder, baking soda, and salt. In a large bowl, using an electric mixer, combine the sugar, applesauce, and oil until creamy. Add the vanilla and mix. Add the coconut milk and half the dry ingredients and mix until just blended. Then add the remaining milk and the other half of the dry ingredients and mix until the batter is just moist—you don't want to overmix. Divide the batter between the prepared pans and spread evenly.

🍮 Bake for 20 to 25 minutes until golden and a toothpick inserted into the center comes out clean. Let cool in the pans on cooling racks for 10 minutes. Run a butter knife around the edge of one of the layers and invert onto another cooling rack. Cool completely before filling and frosting.

🍮 While the cakes are cooling, prepare the custard. In a small saucepan, whisk together the sugar and cornstarch until there are no lumps. Add the coconut milk slowly, whisking to incorporate. Cook over medium heat, whisking constantly, until it begins to lightly boil. Lower the heat and continue to cook for about 10 minutes, whisking, until the mixture begins to thicken and easily coats the back of a spoon. Pour the custard into a heatproof bowl. Let cool to room temperature, periodically whisking to keep it from getting lumpy.

🍮 To assemble the cake, run a butter knife around the edge of one of the layers, invert onto a platter, and peel off the parchment. If needed, level the top of the cake using a cake level or a knife. Spread the custard over the top, starting in the middle and spreading within 1/2 inch of the edge. Remove the other layer from its pan, place on the bottom layer, and level it if you'd like. Carefully spread the buttercream over the sides and top of the cake. (See page 14 for more tips on frosting cakes.) Garnish with flaked coconut, if using.

DIFFICULTY:

SERVINGS: 8 to 10

DAD IS GREAT CHOCOLATE CAKE

If you're not familiar with Bill Cosby's chocolate cake sketch, do me a kindness and Google it. Then, do yourself a bigger kindness and make this cake. It's perfectly decadent, remarkably simple, makes a beautiful presentation, and is not too rich.

INGREDIENTS

1 1/2 cups
all-purpose flour

1 cup
organic granulated sugar

1/3 cup
baking cocoa, sifted

1 teaspoon
baking powder

1/2 teaspoon
baking soda

1/4 teaspoon
salt

1 cup
nondairy milk

1/3 cup
canola or other mild vegetable oil

1 1/2 teaspoons
vanilla extract

1/4 teaspoon
mild vinegar

1 recipe
Chocolate Crème (page 134)

3 tablespoons
crushed chocolate cookies or shaved chocolate for garnish

DIRECTIONS

Preheat the oven to 350°F. Lightly grease a 9 x 5-inch loaf pan and dust with cocoa powder.

In a small bowl, combine the flour, sugar, cocoa, baking powder, baking soda, and salt. In a large bowl, combine the milk, oil, vanilla, and vinegar. Let sit for a few minutes to activate the vinegar. Incorporate half the dry ingredients into the wet ingredients, blending until just mixed, then repeat with the other half. Spread the batter evenly into the prepared pan.

Bake for 40 to 45 minutes, until a toothpick inserted into the center comes out clean. Let cool in the pan on a cooling rack for 15 minutes. Run a butter knife around the edge of the pan and invert onto another cooling rack. Let cool completely before frosting.

To assemble the cake, carefully cut the cake horizontally into thirds using a cake leveler or knife. Spread one-third of the chocolate crème on top of the bottom layer and place the middle layer on top. Spread one-half of the remaining cream on that layer, then place the top layer on. Spread the remaining cream on top of the cake. Garnish with crumbled cookies or chocolate shavings. Store in a sealed container in the refrigerator.

DIFFICULTY:

SERVINGS: 8 to 10

SPUMONI CAKE

This cake flavor was suggested by one of my recipe testers, Lee Ann. Once the idea was in my head, it wouldn't leave. Seriously, spumoni cake? It's brilliant! Chocolate, pistachios, and cherries come together in this cake, only to be topped off with the nectar of the presentation—it's a square layered cake, made by cutting a 9 x 13-inch cake in half. It gives the appearance of a block of ice cream. Fluffy, cakey ice cream . . .

INGREDIENTS

3 cups
all-purpose flour

2 teaspoons
baking powder

1/2 teaspoon
salt

2 cups
organic granulated sugar

2 teaspoons
unsweetened applesauce

1/2 cup
canola or other
mild vegetable oil

1 1/2 cups
nondairy milk

1 teaspoon
vanilla extract

CHOCOLATE ADD-IN

3 tablespoons
nondairy milk

1/4 cup
baking cocoa, sifted

CHERRY ADD-IN

1/3 cup
pureed cherries
(fresh or frozen and thawed)

4 to 5 drops
red food coloring (optional)

PISTACHIO ADD-IN

1/3 cup
finely ground pistachios

2 tablespoons
nondairy milk

4 to 5 drops
green food coloring
(optional)

1 recipe
Cream Cheese Frosting
(page 137)

DIRECTIONS

🍴 Preheat the oven to 350°F. Lightly grease and flour a 9 x 13-inch pan and line with parchment paper, if using. If not using, be sure to grease and flour the bottom well.

🍴 In a medium bowl, combine the flour, baking powder, and salt. In a large bowl, using an electric mixer, combine the sugar, applesauce, and oil and mix until the sugar is thoroughly wet. Add the milk and vanilla and combine well. Incorporate half the dry ingredients into the wet ingredients, blending until just mixed, then repeat with the other half. Divide the batter among three bowls (it doesn't need to be exact, eyeballing it is fine). Combine the chocolate ingredients (milk and cocoa) and gently incorporate into the batter in one of the bowls. Add the cherry puree and red food coloring, if using, to one of the other bowls. Combine the pistachio ingredients (pistachios, milk, and food coloring, if using) and gently incorporate into the final bowl. Drop alternating blobs of batter (about 2/3 cup at a time) into the prepared pan, until all the batter has been added. Using a butter knife, cut through the batter a couple of times to incorporate, but don't overblend.

🍴 Bake for 38 to 43 minutes, until a toothpick inserted into the center comes out clean. The cherry sections will remain slightly more moist, so be sure to check a chocolate or pistachio part. Let cool in the pan on a cooling rack.

🍴 To assemble the cake, cut the cooled cake in half, into 2 pieces 9 x 6.5 inches. You may also like to cut off the edges of the cake, to make the colors visible. Place one of the cake halves on your platter. Level as needed using a cake level or knife. Spread a generous smear of frosting on it and top with the other half of the cake. Spread the remaining frosting on top. Store the leftover cake covered in the refrigerator.

DIFFICULTY:

SERVINGS: 12

BUBBIE'S CHUBBY TUXEDO CAKE

Named after my favorite black-and-white kitteh, this cake will please chocolate and vanilla lovers alike, and for those sandwich cookie folks—over the moon! It's made from a vanilla cake sandwiched between two layers of chocolate cake, all held together with a delicious buttercream frosting, speckled with cookie bits. Soy milk works especially well in this cake, but you may choose another nondairy milk if you wish.

INGREDIENTS

3 cups
all-purpose flour

1 1/2 teaspoons
baking powder

1/2 teaspoon
baking soda

1/4 teaspoon
salt

1/2 cup
canola or other mild vegetable oil

2 cups
organic granulated sugar

1 2/3 cups plus 3 tablespoons
nondairy milk

1/2 teaspoon
mild vinegar

2 teaspoons
vanilla extract

1/4 cup
baking cocoa, sifted

1 1/2 recipes
Vanilla Buttercream (page 139)

1 cup
crushed sandwich cookies
plus extra for decoration

DIRECTIONS

🥄 Preheat the oven to 350°F. Grease and flour 2 (8-inch) round pans and line with parchment paper.

🥄 In a small bowl, combine the flour, baking powder, baking soda, and salt. In a large bowl, preferably using an electric mixer, cream together the oil and sugar until combined. Add the 1 2/3 cups milk, vinegar, and vanilla. Let sit for a few minutes to activate the vinegar. Incorporate half the dry ingredients into the wet ingredients, blending until just mixed, then repeat with the other half. In a small bowl, combine the cocoa powder and the remaining 3 tablespoons milk. Transfer half the batter to another bowl, gently add the cocoa mixture, and mix until just combined. Pour the plain batter into one of the prepared pans and the chocolate batter into the other and spread evenly.

🥄 Bake for 28 to 32 minutes, until a toothpick inserted into the center comes out clean. Let cool in the pans on cooling racks for 15 minutes. Loosen the edges of the cakes with a butter knife and invert onto other cooling racks.

🥄 Make the buttercream as directed and then add the crushed cookies at the end. To assemble the cake, carefully split the chocolate cake in half horizontally. Place the bottom layer on your platter. Add a thick layer of frosting and top with the vanilla cake. If needed, level the top of the cake using a cake level or a knife. Smear another layer of frosting and top with the top chocolate cake layer. Level it if you'd like. Frost the top and sides with the remaining buttercream and decorate with the extra sandwich cookies as desired. Store leftover cake in a sealed container at room temperature.

DIFFICULTY: 🥄🥄🥄

SERVINGS: 12

GLUTEN-FREE MONKEY MAPLE CAKE

Shhh . . . This delectable cake has a moist, flavorful crumb and lovely flavor combination, and no one will ever know it's gluten-free. The combination of maple and banana is heavenly, and it's simple to throw together yet fancy enough to accept lots of praise for making. Don't need gluten-free? Omit the brown rice flour, sorghum flour, tapioca flour, and guar gum and replace with 1 3/4 cups all-purpose flour.

INGREDIENTS

1 cup
brown rice flour

1/2 cup
sorghum flour

1/2 cup
tapioca flour

1 teaspoon
guar gum

1 teaspoon
baking powder

1/2 teaspoon
baking soda

1/4 teaspoon
salt

1/3 cup
melted margarine

1 1/4 cups
organic granulated sugar

2 medium
ripe bananas, mashed, plus 1 or 2 bananas for garnish

3/4 cups
nondairy milk

1 teaspoon
vanilla extract

1 recipe
Maple Buttercream (page 142)

DIRECTIONS

🍤 Preheat the oven to 350°F. Lightly grease and flour 2 (8-inch) round pans and line with parchment paper, if using.

🍤 In a small bowl, combine the brown rice flour, sorghum flour, tapioca flour, guar gum, baking powder, baking soda, and salt. In a large bowl, preferably using an electric mixer, cream together the margarine and sugar until well incorporated and smooth. Add the mashed bananas and mix until combined. Add the milk and vanilla and mix until smooth. Incorporate half the dry ingredients into the wet ingredients, blending until just mixed, then repeat with the other half. Divide the batter between the prepared pans and spread evenly.

🍤 Bake for 24 to 28 minutes, until a toothpick inserted into the center comes out clean. Let cool in the pans on cooling racks for 15 minutes. Loosen the edges of the cakes with a butter knife and invert onto other cooling racks. Cool completely before frosting.

🍤 To assemble the cake, place one of the layers on a platter. If needed, level the top of the cake using a cake level or a knife. Spread with a healthy smear of buttercream and top with slices of the remaining bananas. Place the other layer on the bottom layer and level it if you'd like. Frost the top of the cake with the remaining buttercream. You might have enough left to do some decorating to dress it up. (See page 14 for more tips on frosting cakes.) Store leftover cake in a sealed container in the refrigerator.

DIFFICULTY:

SERVINGS: 8 to 10

SNICKERDOODLE CAKE

Essentially, this is a 'nilla cake recipe. Dressed up with some cinnamon
and a crunchy sugar topping, you have yourself a serious winner.

INGREDIENTS

3 cups
all-purpose flour

1¹/₂ teaspoons
baking powder

¹/₂ teaspoon
baking soda

2 teaspoons plus 1¹/₂ teaspoons
ground cinnamon

¹/₄ teaspoon
salt

¹/₂ cup
canola or other mild vegetable oil

2 cups
organic granulated sugar

3 tablespoons
unsweetened applesauce

1¹/₂ cups plus 1 tablespoon
nondairy milk

¹/₂ teaspoon
mild vinegar

2 teaspoons
vanilla extract

1 recipe
Vanilla Buttercream (page 139)

3 tablespoons
coarse sugar

DIRECTIONS

Preheat the oven to 350°F. Grease and flour 2 (8-inch) round pans and line with parchment paper.

In a small bowl, combine the flour, baking powder, baking soda, the 2 teaspoons cinnamon, and the salt. In a large bowl, preferably using an electric mixer, cream together the oil and sugar until combined. Add the applesauce, milk, vinegar, and vanilla. Incorporate half the dry ingredients into the wet ingredients, blending until just mixed, then repeat with the other half. Divide the batter between the prepared pans and spread evenly.

Bake for 28 to 32 minutes, until a toothpick inserted into the center comes out clean. Let cool in the pans on cooling racks for 15 minutes. Loosen the edges of the cake with a butter knife and invert onto another cooling rack. Cool completely before frosting.

To assemble the cake, place one of the layers on a platter. If needed, level the top of the cake using a cake level or a knife. Spread with a healthy smear of buttercream. Place the other layer on top and level it if you'd like. Frost the sides and top with the remaining buttercream. You might have enough left to do some decorating, so gussy it up! Combine the coarse sugar with the remaining 1¹/₂ teaspoons cinnamon and top the cake with the crunchy mixture. (See page 14 for more tips on frosting cakes.) Store leftover cake covered at room temperature.

DIFFICULTY:

SERVINGS: 10 to 12

MATCHA MADE IN HEAVEN CAKE

Matcha powder is incredible but expensive! Save yourself the heart attack and see if you can get it in bulk so you can minimize the pain to the pocketbook while maximizing the pleasure in your belly. This recipe makes a two-layer cake, but you can make one thick layer, baking it for 38 to 42 minutes.

INGREDIENTS

1¹/² cups
all-purpose flour

1 cup
organic granulated sugar

1 teaspoon
baking powder

1 teaspoon
baking soda

¹/⁴ teaspoon
salt

¹/³ cup
canola or other mild vegetable oil

¹/⁴ cup
unsweetened applesauce

1 cup
nondairy milk

1 teaspoon
matcha powder

1 teaspoon
vanilla extract

1 cup
blueberries plus extra for garnish

1 recipe
Matcha Buttercream (page 141)

DIRECTIONS

🍴 Preheat the oven to 350°F. Lightly grease and flour 2 (8-inch) round pans.

🍴 In a medium bowl, combine the flour, sugar, baking powder, baking soda, and salt. In a large bowl, preferably using an electric mixer, combine the oil and applesauce. Add the milk, matcha, and vanilla and mix until combined. Incorporate half the dry ingredients into the wet ingredients, blending until just mixed, then repeat with the other half. Carefully fold in the blueberries with a spatula. Divide the batter between the prepared pans and spread evenly.

🍴 Bake for 22 to 26 minutes, until golden and a toothpick inserted into the center comes out clean. Let cool completely in the pans on cooling racks.

🍴 To assemble the cake, loosen the edge of one of the layers with a butter knife and place on a platter. If needed, level the top of the cake using a cake level or a knife. Spread the top with a generous helping of buttercream. Remove the other layer from its pan, place on the bottom layer, and level it if you'd like. Frost the top and sides of the cake with the remaining buttercream. (See page 14 for more tips on frosting cakes.) Garnish with blueberries. Store covered at room temperature.

DIFFICULTY: 🥄🥄

SERVINGS: 8 to 10

GERMAN GIRL SCOUT CAKE

Inspired by the classic German Chocolate Cake and the Girl Scouts' Samoa cookies, this cake is a chocolate and coconut lover's dream come true! Lowfat coconut milk is a nice option for the coconut spread.

INGREDIENTS

CAKE

1¹/2 cups
all-purpose flour

1/4 cup
baking cocoa (preferably Dutch processed), sifted

1 cup
organic granulated sugar

1 teaspoon
baking powder

¹/2 teaspoon
baking soda

1/4 teaspoon
salt

1 cup
nondairy milk, at room temperature

1/4 teaspoon
mild vinegar

1/4 cup
chocolate chips, melted

1/4 cup
canola or other mild vegetable oil

1 teaspoon
vanilla extract

COCONUT SPREAD

2 tablespoons
cornstarch

1/3 cup
organic granulated sugar

3/4 cup
nondairy milk

¹/2 teaspoon
vanilla extract

3 cups
unsweetened shredded coconut

1 recipe
Chocolate Ganache (page 133)

DIRECTIONS

- Preheat the oven to 350°F. Grease and flour 2 (8-inch) round pans and line with parchment paper.

- To make the cake, in a small bowl, combine the flour, cocoa, sugar, baking powder, baking soda, and salt. In a large bowl, combine the milk and vinegar and let sit for a few minutes to activate the vinegar. Add the melted chocolate, oil, and vanilla, whisking well. Incorporate half the dry ingredients into the wet ingredients, blending until just mixed, then repeat with the other half. Divide the batter between the prepared pans and spread evenly.

- Bake for 25 to 28 minutes, until a toothpick inserted into the center comes out clean. Let cool in the pans on cooling racks for 10 minutes. Loosen the edges of the cakes with a butter knife and invert onto other cooling racks. Cool completely before frosting.

- To make the spread, in a small saucepan, combine the cornstarch and sugar. Whisk well to break up any lumps. Add the milk and vanilla and whisk thoroughly. Cook over medium heat for about 8 minutes, whisking constantly, until the mixture begins to bubble. Lower the heat and continue stirring until the mixture begins to thicken. Remove from the heat and mix in the coconut until well coated. Let the mixture cool.

- To assemble the cake, place one of the layers on a platter. If needed, level the top of the cake using a cake level or a knife. Cover the top with half of the spread. Drizzle on half of the ganache. Place the other layer on top and level it if you'd like. Cover the top of the cake with the remaining spread and drizzle with the remaining ganache. (See page 14 for more tips on frosting cakes.) Store in a covered container at room temperature.

DIFFICULTY:

SERVINGS: 10 to 12

• • • **CHAPTER 5**

Think Outside the Round Cakes

Cakes need not always be fancy rounds bedazzled with frosting or simple coffee cakes perfect for snacking on. They come in many shapes and sizes, and we're equal opportunity cake-consumers, so no cake is left out!

POUND OF MAPLE SUGAR CAKE

This rich brown sugar pound cake is dense, moist, and delectable. Topped with a delicious maple glaze, what more could you ask for?

INGREDIENTS

2 cups
all-purpose flour

2 teaspoons
baking powder

1/4 teaspoon
salt

1/2 cup
margarine, at room temperature

1 cup
firmly packed brown sugar

1/4 cup
unsweetened applesauce

1/2 cup
nondairy milk

1 tablespoon
molasses

1/2 teaspoon
vanilla extract

1 recipe
Maple Glaze (page 131)

1/2 cup
chopped walnuts (optional)

DIRECTIONS

- Preheat the oven to 325°F. Lightly grease and flour a 9 x 5-inch loaf pan.

- In a small bowl, combine the flour, baking powder, and salt. In a large bowl, cream together the margarine and brown sugar until combined. Add the applesauce, milk, molasses, and vanilla and mix well. Incorporate half the dry ingredients into the wet ingredients, blending until just mixed, then repeat with the other half. Spread the batter evenly into the prepared pan.

- Bake for 42 to 48 minutes, until brown and a toothpick inserted into the center comes out clean. Let cool in the pan on a cooling rack for 20 minutes. Run a butter knife around the edge of the pan and invert onto another cooling rack. Let cool completely before glazing.

- Spread the glaze over the cooled cake and decorate with walnuts, if using. Store loosely covered at room temperature.

DIFFICULTY:

SERVINGS: 10

ORANGE YOU GLAD IT'S PUDDIN' CAKE?

This is one of those simple, delightful recipes that's easy to throw together and is the ultimate comfort food on a cold day. The top gets a light crunch, which gives way to the moist, fragrant cake and creamy pudding bottom.

INGREDIENTS

1 cup
all-purpose flour

1/2 cup plus 1/4 cup
organic granulated sugar

1/2 teaspoon
baking powder

1/4 teaspoon
baking soda

a scant sprinkle
salt

1/4 cup
margarine, melted

1/2 cup
nondairy milk, warmed

1 medium
orange, zested, plus 1/2 cup juice

1 1/2 teaspoons
vanilla extract

1 tablespoon
cornstarch

1 cup
boiling water

powdered sugar for dusting

DIRECTIONS

Preheat the oven to 350°F. Lightly grease and flour an 8-inch square pan or other small baking dish.

To make the cake, in a small bowl, combine the flour, the 1/2 cup sugar, the baking powder, baking soda, and salt. Make a well in the middle of the flour mixture and add the margarine, milk, orange zest, and vanilla. Mix until just combined. Spread the batter evenly into the prepared pan. It will seem like there isn't much batter; this is normal. In a small bowl, combine the remaining 1/4 cup sugar and the cornstarch until there are no lumps. Sprinkle this over the top of the batter. In a small bowl, combine the orange juice and water and pour over the top of the batter. Do not stir. At this point you will question whether I'm crazy.

Bake for 30 to 40 minutes. Check an 8-inch square pan after 30 minutes; wait a few minutes longer for a smaller pan. The cake will have risen to the top of the pan and will be lightly brown. The pudding layer will be bubbling up around the sides, and when moved the cake will appear to float. Let the warm cake sit in the pan on a cooling rack for 15 minutes before serving, to let the pudding thicken. Serve with a sprinkle of powdered sugar. This cake is best served warmed the day it's made.

DIFFICULTY:

SERVINGS: 6

GLUTEN-FREE LEMON POPPY CHEESECAKE

This cheesecake can easily be made gluten-free or not, depending on the kind of cookies you buy for the bottom. It's light and creamy and delicious, and I dare any nonvegan to smite its name—this is a cheesecake to be reckoned with. If you want to make it really thick, you can double the filling and bake for an additional 15 minutes. Like all cheesecakes, this is best made the day before you wish to serve it.

INGREDIENTS

GRAHAM CRACKER CRUST

1 1/4 cups
crushed graham cracker or ginger cookie crumbs

1 tablespoon
organic granulated sugar

2 tablespoons
melted margarine

FILLING

1 (12-ounce) package
aseptic firm tofu

1 (8-ounce) container
soy cream cheese

3/4 cup
organic granulated sugar

2 medium
lemons, zested

1/4 cup
lemon juice

1 tablespoon
cornstarch

1/2 teaspoon
vanilla extract

1 tablespoon
poppy seeds

RASPBERRY TOPPING

1/4 cup
organic granulated sugar

1 tablespoon
cornstarch

1 1/4 cups
raspberries

1 tablespoon
water

DIRECTIONS

🍃 Preheat the oven to 350°F. Lightly grease and flour an 8-inch springform pan.

🍃 To make the crust, in a small bowl, combine the cookie crumbs and sugar. Add the margarine and combine until the mixture resembles coarse sand. Press the crust into the bottom of the prepared pan and bake for 10 minutes. Remove from the oven and let cool.

🍃 To make the filling, in the bowl of a food processor or blender, add the tofu, cream cheese, and sugar. Process until mostly incorporated. Add the lemon zest and juice, cornstarch, and vanilla and process, scraping down the sides as needed, until the mixture is creamy and smooth. Add the poppy seeds and mix by hand (you don't want to pulverize them). Spread the mixture evenly over the crust and return the pan to the oven.

🍃 Bake for 40 to 45 minutes. The top should look set up and almost like it has a skin on it, but the cake should still jiggle a little if tapped. Let cool to room temperature in the pan on a cooling rack before transferring to the refrigerator.

🍃 To make the topping, in a small saucepan, combine the sugar and cornstarch. Add the raspberries and water. Mix until incorporated and cook on medium-low heat until the raspberries soften and release their juices. Mash them lightly with the back of a fork and continue to cook, stirring often, about 8 minutes, until the sugar and cornstarch dissolve and the mixture is thick and bubbly. Remove from the heat and let cool to room temperature, stirring occasionally, before spreading over the cheesecake. Store the cake covered overnight in the refrigerator. Remove the springform ring before serving.

DIFFICULTY:

SERVINGS: 12

PLUMPY PUMPKIN ROLL

Moist, pumpkiny cake and creamy filling make this the envy of all the sugar pumpkins in the neighborhood. This pumpkin roll is much easier to make than it looks, but it does require that you are attentive to the directions. Be sure to read ahead of time the technique for rolling it so you can be fast on your feet; then, you should be all set. What's great about this roll is that you can make it a day or two before you need it and stow it away in the refrigerator for fast and fabulous munching. Enjoy with a warm cup of chai . . . total perfection.

INGREDIENTS

CAKE

3/4 cup
all-purpose flour

1 teaspoon
ground cinnamon

1/2 teaspoon
baking powder

1/4 teaspoon
baking soda

1/4 teaspoon
ground ginger

a sprinkle
salt

3/4 cup
canned pumpkin puree
(not pumpkin pie filling)

2/3 cup
organic granulated sugar

3 tablespoons
canola or other mild vegetable oil

1/4 teaspoon
vanilla extract

1/4 cup
powdered sugar

CREAM CHEESE FILLING

1 (8-ounce) container
soy cream cheese, at room temperature

3 tablespoons
margarine, at room temperature

1 1/2 cups
powdered sugar, sifted

1 teaspoon
vanilla extract

DIRECTIONS

Preheat the oven to 350°F. Lightly grease the sides of an 11 x 15-inch jelly roll pan and line the bottom with parchment paper. Parchment is a necessity for this recipe. If you don't have a jelly roll pan, you can still make this with a 9 x 13-inch pan, but you will need to increase the baking time by a few minutes because the cake will be thicker.

To make the cake, in a small bowl, combine the flour, cinnamon, baking powder, baking soda, ginger, and salt. In a medium bowl, combine the pumpkin and sugar until creamy and well mixed. Add the oil and vanilla and mix until well blended. Incorporate half the dry ingredients into the wet ingredients, blending until just mixed, then repeat with the other half. Carefully spread the batter evenly into the prepared pan (an offset spatula is great for this). If using the jelly roll pan, the batter will be spread very thin.

Bake for 13 to 15 minutes, a little longer for a 9 x 13-inch pan, until the cake is puffy and a toothpick inserted into the center comes out clean. We are going to wrap this cake up in a towel directly from the oven to create the dense crumb and natural curve needed for a rolled cake. This is not hard, but to ensure success, read the next step a couple of times if you've never tried this technique before.

While the cake is baking, prepare a clean dish towel (that is at least the size of your pan) by sprinkling it with the powdered sugar. Once the cake is done, immediately loosen the edges of the cake with a butter knife and invert onto the prepared towel, near an edge. The top of the cake should be face down. Peel off the parchment. Carefully wrap up the cake in the towel, rolling from the long side (you want a longer, skinnier roll, rather than a shorter, fatter one). A large part of the towel will be wrapped inside the spiral of the cake. Let the towel-wrapped cake cool completely on a cooling rack.

👩‍🍳 While the cake is cooling, in a large bowl, preferably with an electric mixer, prepare the filling by creaming together the cream cheese and margarine. Add the powdered sugar and vanilla and mix until creamy. Store in the freezer to firm up, no longer than 1 hour, until ready to use. You want to make sure the cream is firm, but still easy to spread.

👩‍🍳 To assemble the cake, ready a piece of plastic wrap big enough to wrap around your roll. Carefully unroll the cooled cake and gently spread the filling along the inside (top) of the roll, all the way to the edge. Reroll the cake, without the towel, and carefully transfer to the plastic wrap. Roll the cake in wrap and then add a layer of tinfoil to help provide stability. Store the cake in the refrigerator for at least 2 hours before serving. Serve cold. Store leftover cake, wrapped, in the refrigerator.

DIFFICULTY:

SERVINGS: 10 to 12 (2 slices per serving)

GLUTEN-FREE BERRY SHORTCAKE

For shortcake, you coat your flour with cold fat (margarine) before adding liquid, to keep the crumb tender by preventing gluten from forming. It's a perfect treat for baking gluten-free! Add the fresh berries and amazing coconut cream topping and you'll be in summer heaven. Don't need gluten-free? Omit the brown rice flour and tapioca starch and replace with 1 cup all-purpose flour.

INGREDIENTS

3 cups
chopped fresh berries, such as strawberries, blueberries, or raspberries

1 tablespoon plus ¼ cup
organic granulated sugar

1 cup
gluten-free oats, coarsely ground

1 cup
brown rice flour

¼ cup
tapioca starch

1 teaspoon
baking powder

1 teaspoon
baking soda

¼ teaspoon
salt

½ cup
cold margarine, cut into pieces

½ cup
nondairy milk

1 recipe
Coconut Cream Topping (page 136)

DIRECTIONS

🥄 In a medium bowl, combine the berries and the 1 tablespoon sugar. Cover and let sit in the refrigerator for at least 1 hour to macerate.

🥄 Preheat the oven to 350°F. Lightly grease an 8-inch round pan and dust with gluten-free flour.

🥄 In a food processor or a large bowl, combine the oats, brown rice flour, tapioca starch, the remaining ¼ cup sugar, the baking powder, baking soda, and salt. Add the margarine in chunks, cutting it into the flour by pulsing or with a fork, until the mixture is coarse. Slowly pour in the milk until the mixture comes together into a sticky batter. Spread the batter evenly in the prepared pan.

🥄 Bake for 20 to 25 minutes, until lightly golden and a toothpick inserted into the center comes out clean. Let cool in the pan on a cooling rack. Serve with the berries and the cream.

DIFFICULTY:

SERVINGS: 8

LOVELY LEMON POUND CAKE

This recipe makes one tall, full loaf of pound cake and a nummy side of berry compote. Perfect for sharing, it's a potluck hit, for sure.

INGREDIENTS

2 cups
all-purpose flour

2 teaspoons
baking powder

1/2 teaspoon
baking soda

1/4 teaspoon
salt

2 small
lemons, zested and juiced

3/4 cup
nondairy milk

1 teaspoon
vanilla extract

1/4 cup
margarine, at room temperature

1/2 (8-ounce) container
soy cream cheese

1 cup
organic granulated sugar

1 recipe
Berry Compote (page 137)

DIRECTIONS

🐷 Preheat the oven to 350°F. Lightly grease and flour a 9 x 5-inch loaf pan.

🐷 In a medium bowl, combine the flour, baking powder, baking soda, and salt. In a small bowl, combine the lemon zest and juice, milk, and vanilla. Let sit for a few minutes to activate the lemon juice. In a large bowl, preferably using an electric mixer, cream together the margarine and cream cheese until combined. Add the sugar and mix well. Add the milk mixture to the margarine mixture and combine. Incorporate half the dry ingredients into the wet ingredients, blending until just mixed, then repeat with the other half. Spread the batter evenly into the prepared pan.

🐷 Bake for 42 to 47 minutes, until a toothpick inserted into the center comes out clean and the loaf is lightly browned. Let cool in the pan on a cooling rack. Serve slices of the cake with the berry compote. Store covered, at room temperature.

DIFFICULTY LEVEL:

SERVINGS: 10

GLUTEN-FREE PERFECT PB BROWNIE CHEESECAKE

Brownies. Peanut Butter. Chocolate. Cheesecake. It's too much to handle! This cheesecake has the potential to bring an abundance of joy to everyone you share it with. The question is: Will you share? Don't need gluten-free? Omit the chickpea flour, brown rice flour, tapioca flour, and guar gum and replace with 1/2 cup all-purpose flour.

INGREDIENTS

BROWNIE CRUST

1/3 cup
chickpea flour

1/4 cup
organic granulated sugar

2 tablespoons
brown rice flour

2 tablespoons
tapioca starch

2 tablespoons
baking cocoa

1/4 teaspoon
baking powder

1/8 teaspoon
guar gum

a pinch
salt

3 tablespoons
margarine, at room temperature

1/3 cup
unsweetened applesauce

1/4 cup
nondairy milk

FILLING

1 (12-ounce) package
aseptic firm tofu

1 (8-ounce) container
soy cream cheese

3/4 cup
organic granulated sugar

3/4 cup
natural peanut butter

1 teaspoon
lemon juice

1 teaspoon
vanilla extract

1/4 cup
melted dark chocolate

DIRECTIONS

🥄 Preheat the oven to 350°F. Lightly grease and flour an 8- or 9-inch springform pan.

🥄 To make the crust, in a small bowl, combine the chickpea flour, sugar, brown rice flour, tapioca starch, cocoa, baking powder, guar gum, and salt. In a large bowl, preferably with an electric mixer, cream together the margarine and applesauce until smooth. Add the milk and mix in. Incorporate half the dry ingredients into the wet ingredients, blending just until mixed, then repeat with the other half. Spread the batter evenly into the prepared pan and bake for 10 minutes. Remove and let cool.

🥄 To make the filling, in the bowl of a food processor or blender, add the tofu, cream cheese, and sugar. Process until mostly blended. Add the peanut butter, lemon juice, and vanilla, scraping down the sides as needed, until the mixture is creamy and smooth. Transfer one-half of the mixture to another bowl and reserve, then add the melted chocolate and mix until well incorporated. Alternate the plain peanut butter mixture with the chocolate peanut butter mixture side by side on top of the crust and swirl with a knife.

🥄 Bake for 40 to 45 minutes. The top should look set and almost like it has a "skin" on it, but the cake should still jiggle a little if tapped. Let cool to room temperature in the pan on a cooling rack. Remove the springform rim before serving. Store covered in the refrigerator.

DIFFICULTY:

SERVINGS: 12

TASTES GREAT FRUITCAKE

Ah, fruitcake. The butt of many a holiday joke. But no one will give you a hard time about this light cake, studded with dried fruit and nuts. They'll be too busy stuffing their faces with it. This version is a bit less, um, brilliant than the traditional neon candied cherries version, but you can feel free to substitute the dried fruit with those familiar favorites if you'd like. The added bonus is that these cakes don't need to cure, so you don't have to start working on them in October to enjoy their Yuletide cheer! You can customize this cake to match your holiday traditions. Add candied orange or orange zest or dark liquor and some molasses in place of the vanilla if you are used to heavier, darker cakes.

INGREDIENTS

1 cup
all-purpose flour

2 tablespoons
organic granulated sugar

1/2 teaspoon
baking powder

1/8 teaspoon
salt

1/3 cup
agave nectar

1/2 cup
orange juice, or 1/4 cup orange juice
and 1/4 cup rum or bandy if you're
going for the boozy taste

2 tablespoons
applesauce

2 tablespoons
canola or other mild vegetable oil

1 teaspoon
vanilla extract

1/2 cup
chopped nuts, such as walnuts
or pecans

1/2 cup
chopped sweet dried fruit,
such as dates, figs, raisins

1/2 cup
chopped tart dried fruit,
such as apricots, candied orange
peel, tart cherries

1/3 cup
apple cider or alcohol (same as
used in batter) for soaking

DIRECTIONS

🥄 Preheat the oven to 325°F. Lightly grease and flour 1 (9 x 5-inch) loaf pan or 4 (2½ x 4-inch) mini loaf pans.

🥄 In a small bowl, combine the flour, sugar, baking powder, and salt. In a medium bowl, combine the agave, orange juice, applesauce, oil, and vanilla. Whisk until combined. Incorporate half the dry ingredients into the wet ingredients, blending just until mixed, then repeat with the other half. Add the nuts and dried fruit and mix until just combined. Divide the batter between the prepared pans and spread evenly.

🥄 Bake mini cakes for 24 to 28 minutes, a full loaf for 45 to 50 minutes, until lightly golden and a toothpick inserted into the center comes out clean. Remove from the oven and set the pans on cooling racks. While warm, poke the cake randomly with a toothpick to create pinholes. Slowly and evenly pour the apple cider or remaining alcohol over the cakes, allowing it time to be absorbed. Let cool in the pan on the cooling rack for 20 minutes. Loosen the edges of the cake with a butter knife and invert onto another cooling rack. Let cool to room temperature. Store wrapped or in a sealed container in the refrigerator.

DIFFICULTY:

YIELD: 1 large loaf or 4 mini loaves

CHAPTER 6

No-Bake Cakes

Cake . . . but not from an oven. Impossible, you say? Think again!
Using your trusty rice cooker, slow cooker, or even a stovetop pot,
you can make delicious cakes in as little as 30 minutes, or you can
let the aroma fill your house over the course of a day if you slow cook
a cake for dessert. Anything goes with these unbaked beauties!

SPICED-RICE CRANBERRY CAKE

While it doesn't contain any rice, this is a simple treat that goes straight from the rice cooker to your table in under 1 hour. The cake holds up beautifully, and the spices really continue to develop, so leftovers are perfect.

INGREDIENTS

1 1/2 cups
all-purpose flour

3/4 cup
organic granulated sugar

1 teaspoon
ground cinnamon

1/2 teaspoon
ground ginger

1/4 teaspoon
ground nutmeg

2 teaspoons
baking powder

1/4 teaspoon
salt

1/3 cup
unsweetened applesauce

1/4 cup
canola or other mild vegetable oil

1/2 cup
nondairy milk

1/2 teaspoon
vanilla extract

2/3 cup
chopped cranberries,
preferably fresh or frozen,
or 1/3 cup dried

1 recipe
Basic Glaze (page 130)

DIRECTIONS

Lightly grease the inside of your rice cooker pot.

In a small bowl, combine the flour, sugar, cinnamon, ginger, nutmeg, baking powder, and salt. In a large bowl, combine the applesauce and oil. Add the milk and vanilla and mix until combined. Incorporate half the dry ingredients into the wet ingredients, blending until just mixed, then repeat with the other half. Gently stir in the cranberries. Spread the batter evenly into the rice cooker pot.

If your rice cooker is very basic, just select start. If you have more options, cook on the setting you would use to make white rice. Cook for 30 to 35 minutes, until a toothpick inserted into the center comes out clean. If the toothpick doesn't come out clean, let it cook for 5 minutes longer and check again. Remove the pot from the rice cooker and let the cake cool in the pot on a cooling rack. Once the cake is completely cool, run a butter knife around the edge of the cake and invert onto a platter. Pour the glaze over the cake and let it sit for 10 minutes to set. Store leftover cake loosely covered at room temperature.

DIFFICULTY:

SERVINGS: 8 to 10

BLACK FOREST CROCK CAKE

This is another recipe to rescue you when your schedule is packed . . . or you've just become addicted to a TV saga and streaming episodes of said show has consumed your life. Not that that happens to me. I'm just saying. One-bowl cake recipes never hurt a *LOST* marathon.

INGREDIENTS

1¹/₂ **cups**
all-purpose flour

¹/₄ **cup**
baking cocoa, sifted

³/₄ **cup**
organic granulated sugar

1¹/₂ **teaspoons**
baking powder

¹/₂ **teaspoon**
baking soda

¹/₄ **teaspoon**
salt

³/₄ **cup plus 2 tablespoons**
nondairy milk

¹/₄ **cup**
canola or other mild vegetable oil

1 **teaspoon**
vanilla extract

¹/₃ **cup**
chocolate chips

1 **(21-ounce) can**
cherry pie filling

DIRECTIONS

- Lightly grease the pan inside a 4- to 5-quart slow cooker.

- In a large bowl, combine the flour, cocoa, sugar, baking powder, baking soda, and salt. Mix well to combine. Create a well in the middle of the mixture and add the milk, oil, and vanilla. Combine the mixture until it is just mixed. Add the chocolate chips and then swirl in the cherry pie filling; you don't want to incorporate it completely, but to leave it more like a swirl. Spread the batter evenly into the slow cooker.

- Cook with the lid on for 5 to 6 hours on low heat, or for 2¹/₂ to 3 hours on high. Warning: Because this cake is dark, if the inside of your slow cooker is also dark, you may get some blackening on the edges if you cook on high heat. Condensation from the lid can cause the center of the cake to look uncooked, even when it's done, so don't be deceived.

- The cake is done when a toothpick inserted into the center comes out clean, with no cake crumbs (there might be some juice from the cherries). Remove the container from the slow cooker base and let it cool on a cooling rack. This cake is best served warm, from the slow cooker dish, but it holds up fairly well overnight. Store covered in the refrigerator.

DIFFICULTY:

SERVINGS: 12

NECKING WITH BLUEBERRIES SLUMP

Blueberries and nectarines, sitting in a pot—racy, no? A slump (otherwise known as a grunt, but that sounds too gross for me) is made on the stovetop by cooking up some fruit and adding the batter. Be sure you have a pot with a tightly fitted lid, as the heat steams the cake on top, making a delicious and fast treat that you can easily justify eating for breakfast. It's not that much different from pancakes . . . although it *does* taste better with a scoop of ice cream.

INGREDIENTS

2 tablespoons
canola or other mild vegetable oil, divided

2 cups
blueberries

4 ripe
nectarines, sliced

1/2 cup
organic granulated sugar, divided

1/2 cup
all-purpose flour

1/4 cup
cornmeal

1/2 teaspoon
baking powder

a pinch
salt

1/3 cup
nondairy milk

DIRECTIONS

🥄 In a medium pot with a tight-fitting lid, heat 1 tablespoon of the oil on medium heat. Add the blueberries, nectarines, and 1/4 cup of the sugar. Cook, stirring often, for 10 to 15 minutes, until the fruit releases its juices and the nectarines soften.

🥄 In a small bowl, combine the remaining 1/4 cup sugar, the flour, cornmeal, baking powder, and salt. Add the milk and the remaining 1 tablespoon oil and mix until just combined. Spoon the batter on top of the fruit mixture. The batter might look sparse, and if it doesn't cover the whole thing, that's fine, as it will expand while cooking.

🥄 Cover the pot with the lid and lower the heat to medium-low. Cook, without removing the lid, for 15 minutes. When done, remove the lid and remove the pot from the heat. Scoop and serve immediately.

DIFFICULTY:

SERVINGS: 6

MOCHA MELT CAKE, TWO WAYS

You're about to sit down to dinner and think, "Mmm . . . I wish we had dessert." Never fear—in 30 minutes your friendly rice cooker will have such a treat ready and waiting for you with no need to heat the oven or grease any pans. Depending on the size of your rice cooker, you can "undercook" this cake for a giant molten lava cake or you can cook it all the way to fluffy perfection. Try it both ways!

INGREDIENTS

CAKE

1 cup
all-purpose flour

2/3 cup
organic granulated sugar

3 tablespoons
baking cocoa (preferably Dutch processed), sifted

1 1/2 teaspoons
baking powder

1/2 teaspoon
baking soda

1/4 teaspoon
salt

1/2 cup
nondairy milk

3 tablespoons
canola or other mild vegetable oil

1/2 teaspoon
vanilla extract

1/3 cup
chocolate chips

MOCHA SYRUP

3 tablespoons
baking cocoa (preferably Dutch processed), sifted

3 tablespoons
organic granulated sugar

2 teaspoons
instant coffee granules

2/3 cup
hot water (almost boiling, but not quite)

DIRECTIONS

🐾 Spray the inside of the rice cooker pot with nonstick spray.

🐾 To make the cake, in a large bowl combine the flour, sugar, cocoa, baking powder, baking soda, and salt. Make a well in the mixture and add the milk, oil, and vanilla. Mix until just combined; it will be thick like brownie batter. Spread the batter evenly in the rice cooker and sprinkle the top with the chocolate chips.

🐾 To make the syrup, in a small, heat-resistant bowl, combine the cocoa, sugar, and coffee. Add the hot water and whisk until the coffee is dissolved and there are no lumps. Pour the hot liquid over the top of the cake. Do not stir.

🐾 If your rice cooker is very basic, just select start. If you have more options, cook on the setting you would use to make white rice. For a fluffy, finished cake, cook for 30 to 35 minutes, until a toothpick inserted into the center comes out clean. For a lava cake, check after 20 minutes; the outer edges and top should be set, but the middle still very moist.

🐾 For the fully cooked cake, when the rice cooker alarm sounds that it is done, remove the pot from the rice cooker and let cool for 15 minutes on a cooling rack. Gently loosen the cake with the edge of a rubber spatula or other nonmetal utensil, and invert onto a serving platter. Serve warm with ice cream or Coconut Cream Topping (page 136) and you surely will have many friends.

🐾 For the molten cake, remove the pot from the rice cooker and let cool for 10 minutes on a cooling rack. You will need to scoop the cake out of the pot with a large spoon, but no one will complain, I promise. The finished cake is best eaten the day of, but it does keep. Store leftover fully cooked cake in a covered container at room temperature. The molten cake should be eaten the day of making.

DIFFICULTY: 🥄🥄

SERVINGS: 8 to 10

SLOW AS APPLE PIE CAKE

Scenario 1: It's hot. You don't want to use your oven, but you want cake. Scenario 2: It's one of those lazy days. You want to make a cake for after dinner but don't want to deal with it. This cake is the answer in both cases. You simply dump the batter into your slow cooker, let it go, and there you are, with a fluffy, moist, delicious cake. There's an apple filling on the bottom that keeps you from having to worry about any frosting/icing/decorating nonsense. It takes 5 to 6 hours to cook on low, depending on the size of your cooker, so plan ahead. This recipe goes against one of my usual tenets of baking: canned pie filling. But, the objective here is delicious cake with minimal effort, and you know what? It works.

INGREDIENTS

1 1/2 cups
all-purpose flour

3/4 cup
organic granulated sugar

2 teaspoons
baking powder

1 teaspoon
ground cinnamon

1/4 teaspoon
salt

3/4 cup plus 2 tablespoons
nondairy milk

1/4 cup
canola or other mild vegetable oil

1/2 teaspoon
vanilla extract

2 (21-ounce) cans
apple pie filling

DIRECTIONS

- Spray the pan inside a 4- to 5-quart slow cooker with nonstick spray.

- In a bowl, combine the flour, sugar, baking powder, cinnamon, and salt. Whisk to combine. Create a well in the middle of the dry ingredients and add the milk, oil, and vanilla. Whisk until just incorporated. Spread the apple pie filling in the cooker. Spread the cake batter evenly over the apples.

- Cook on low for 5 to 5 1/2 hours, or on high for 2 to 2 1/2 hours, until a toothpick inserted into the center comes out clean of batter (the apples will cause some unavoidable moisture on the toothpick) and the top of the cake springs back when touched. Condensation from the lid can cause the center of the cake to look uncooked, even when it is cooked, so don't be deceived. Once baked, turn the slow cooker off and remove the pan from the unit. Let cool in the pan on a cooling rack for at least 20 minutes before serving. Scoop the cake and apple bottom from the pan with a large spoon. Serve warm with ice cream. Store leftover cake in a covered container in the refrigerator. This cake keeps remarkably well, especially for being baked in a slow cooker.

DIFFICULTY:

SERVINGS: 12

GLUTEN-FREE SLUMP INTO FALL

This slump combines the delicious texture of apples and pears with a lightly spiced cake that is fluffy and gluten-free. Don't need gluten-free? Omit the sorghum flour, tapioca starch, and guar gum and replace with 3/4 cup plus 2 tablespoons all-purpose flour.

INGREDIENTS

2 tablespoons
canola or other mild vegetable oil, divided

5 to 6 cups
peeled 1/2-inch slices apples and pears (about 1 1/2 pounds)

1/2 cup
organic granulated sugar, divided

3/4 cups
sorghum flour

1/4 cup
tapioca starch

1/2 teaspoon
ground cinnamon

1/4 teaspoon
guar gum

1/4 teaspoon
baking powder

1/4 teaspoon
baking soda

1/8 teaspoon
salt

1/2 cup plus 2 tablespoons
nondairy milk

1/2 teaspoon
lemon juice

1 teaspoon
vanilla extract

DIRECTIONS

🌱 In a medium pot with a tight-fitting lid, heat 1 tablespoon of the oil on medium heat. Add the apples and pears and 1/4 cup of the sugar. Cook, stirring often, for 10 to 15 minutes, until the fruit begins to soften.

🌱 In a small bowl, combine the remaining 1/4 cup sugar, the sorghum flour, tapioca starch, cinnamon, guar gum, baking powder, baking soda, and salt. Add the milk, the remaining 1 tablespoon oil, the lemon juice, and the vanilla and mix until just combined. Spoon scoops of the batter on top of the fruit mixture. The batter might look sparse and if it doesn't cover the whole thing, that's fine, as it will expand while cooking.

🌱 Cover with the lid and lower the heat to medium-low. Without removing the lid, cook for 15 minutes, or until a toothpick inserted into the center comes out clean. When done, remove the lid and remove the pot from the heat. Scoop and serve immediately.

DIFFICULTY:

SERVINGS: 6

CHAPTER 7

Cake Accoutrements

Every cake needs some topping, sometimes. Every cake needs some filling, somehow . . . And here those needs and wishes are satisfied, with a wide array of fillings, frostings, and toppings that you can mix and match with any cake for an endless variety of treats!

BASIC GLAZE
Makes: $1/8$ to $1/4$ cup

INGREDIENTS

3/4 to 1¼ cups
powdered sugar, sifted

1 to 2 teaspoons
nondairy milk

DIRECTIONS

In a small bowl, whisk the powdered sugar into the milk, starting with smaller increments, adding more as needed to make a creamy, lightly spreadable glaze.

CINNAMON GLAZE
Makes: $1/8$ to ¼ cup

INGREDIENTS

2 tablespoons
nondairy milk

1 teaspoon
cinnamon

1½ to 2 cups
powdered sugar, sifted

DIRECTIONS

In a medium bowl, combine the milk with the cinnamon. Whisk in the powdered sugar until thick enough to coat a spoon but thin enough to drizzle.

MAPLE GLAZE
Makes: $1/8$ to $1/4$ cup

INGREDIENTS

1 tablespoon
nondairy milk

$1/2$ teaspoon
vanilla extract

$3/4$ teaspoon
maple extract

1 to $1^{1/2}$ cups
powdered sugar, sifted

DIRECTIONS

In a medium bowl, combine the milk, vanilla extract, and maple extract. Whisk in the powdered sugar until the glaze reaches a smooth consistency.

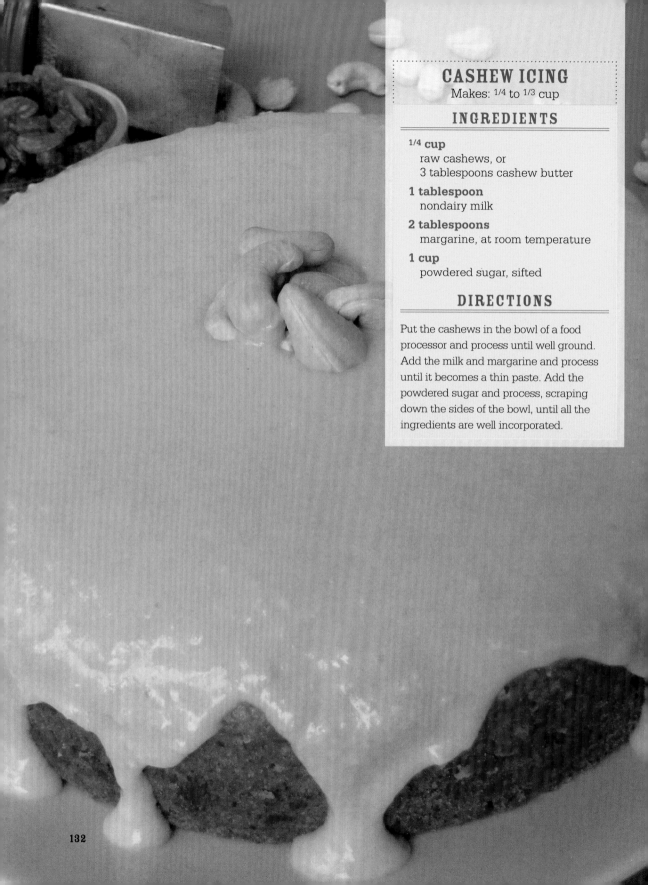

CASHEW ICING

Makes: 1/4 to 1/3 cup

INGREDIENTS

1/4 cup
raw cashews, or
3 tablespoons cashew butter

1 tablespoon
nondairy milk

2 tablespoons
margarine, at room temperature

1 cup
powdered sugar, sifted

DIRECTIONS

Put the cashews in the bowl of a food processor and process until well ground. Add the milk and margarine and process until it becomes a thin paste. Add the powdered sugar and process, scraping down the sides of the bowl, until all the ingredients are well incorporated.

CHOCOLATE GANACHE
Makes: 1/2 cup

INGREDIENTS

1/3 cup
chocolate chips or chopped dark chocolate

1 tablespoon
margarine

2 tablespoons
nondairy milk

DIRECTIONS

Place the chocolate, margarine, and milk in a small saucepan and cook over medium-low heat, stirring often, until melted. Remove from the heat and let cool.

CHOCOLATE SAUCE
Makes: 2/3 cup

INGREDIENTS

1/2 cup
chopped dark chocolate

3 tablespoons
nondairy milk

1 tablespoon
margarine

DIRECTIONS

Combine the chocolate, milk, and margarine in a double boiler over barely simmering water and melt until smooth. If you don't have a double boiler, put 1 to 2 inches of water in a pot and place a heatproof bowl over it, making sure the bottom of the bowl is suspended over the water. Remove from the heat. Use the sauce warm.

CHOCOLATE CRÈME

Makes: 2 1/4 cups

INGREDIENTS

1 1/4 cups
chocolate chips

1 (12-ounce) package
firm silken aseptic tofu,
at room temperature

2 tablespoons
brown rice syrup
or agave nectar

1/4 teaspoon
vanilla extract

DIRECTIONS

In a double boiler over barely simmering
water, melt the chocolate until smooth,
stirring often. If you don't have a double
boiler, put 1 to 2 inches of water in a pot
and place a heatproof bowl over it, making
sure the bottom of the bowl is suspended
over the water.

In the bowl of a food processor or blender,
crumble the tofu. Blend for about 30
seconds, until fairly smooth. Add the melted
chocolate, brown rice syrup, and vanilla
and blend until well incorporated, scraping
down the bowl or canister as needed.
Transfer the crème to a container and chill
in the refrigerator for at least 1 hour.

RASPBERRY CRÈME
Makes: 2 cups

INGREDIENTS

1 (12-ounce) package
aseptic firm tofu

1 cup
fresh or thawed
frozen raspberries

1/3 cup
organic granulated sugar

1/2 teaspoon
vanilla extract

DIRECTIONS

In a food processor or blender, combine the tofu, raspberries, sugar, and vanilla. Puree, scraping down the sides of the bowl, for about 2 minutes, until smooth. Transfer to a container and chill in the refrigerator for at least 1 hour.

COCONUT CREAM TOPPING
Makes: 1 cup
An all-purpose cream topping to woo your friends and family.

INGREDIENTS

1 (13½-ounce) can
regular coconut milk (not low-fat),
refrigerated for at least 3 hours

½ cup
powdered sugar

¼ teaspoon
vanilla extract

DIRECTIONS

Chill a bowl and the beaters from an electric mixer in the freezer for 15 minutes. Remove the coconut milk from the refrigerator and remove the entire lid from the can. Scoop out the coconut cream from the can (do not include the liquid) and add to the chilled bowl. Add the powdered sugar and vanilla and whip until creamy. Store in the refrigerator. Serve cold.

CREAM CHEESE FROSTING
Makes: 1 1/4 to 1 1/2 cups

INGREDIENTS

1/2 (8-ounce) container
soy cream cheese

2 tablespoons
margarine, at room temperature

1/2 teaspoon
vanilla extract

1 to 1 1/2 cups
powdered sugar, sifted

DIRECTIONS

In a medium bowl, using an electric mixer, combine the cream cheese and margarine until smooth. Add the vanilla and mix in. Add the powdered sugar, 1/2 cup at a time, until the frosting is the desired sweetness and consistency.

BERRY COMPOTE
Makes: 2 cups

INGREDIENTS

2 teaspoons
cornstarch

1/4 cup
organic granulated sugar

2 cups
mixed berries, roughly chopped

2 tablespoons
water

DIRECTIONS

In a medium pot, combine the cornstarch and sugar and whisk until any lumps are gone. Add the berries and water and cook on medium heat, stirring often, until the berries release their juices and the sugar dissolves. Once the mixture begins to bubble and spit, reduce the heat to medium-low and continue to stir for about 10 minutes, until the berries break down and the compote begins to thicken. You can crush the berries with a potato masher if you'd like it to be less chunky. Once the mixture coats the back of a spoon and the cornstarch and sugar are well dissolved, remove from the heat.

CINNAMON CREAM CHEESE FROSTING

Makes: 1¼ to 1½ cups

INGREDIENTS

1 (8-ounce) container
soy cream cheese, at room temperature

2 tablespoons
margarine, at room temperature

2 to 3 cups
powdered sugar

1 to 2 teaspoons
ground cinnamon

1 tablespoon
nondairy milk

DIRECTIONS

In a medium bowl, using an electric mixer, blend the cream cheese and margarine together until smooth. Sift 1 cup powdered sugar and 1 teaspoon cinnamon into the cream cheese mixture, blending until smooth. Gradually add the milk and the remaining sugar and cinnamon until a smooth but spreadable mixture is achieved. The cinnamon flavor becomes more prominent as the frosting sits, so err on the side of caution—you don't want your frosting to taste like a stick of Big Red!

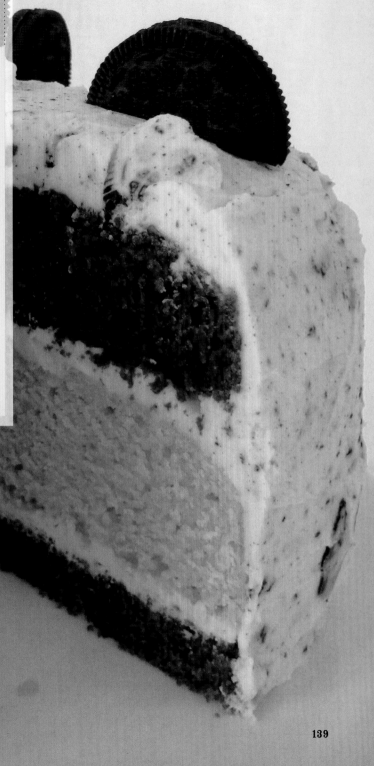

VANILLA BUTTERCREAM
Makes: 1 1/2 cups

A fabulous all-purpose recipe, this makes a
great frosting and, with a little less sugar, a
decadent filling.

INGREDIENTS

1/2 cup
margarine, at room temperature

1/2 cup
shortening, at room temperature

1 teaspoon
vanilla extract

3 to 4 cups
powdered sugar, sifted

a splash
nondairy milk, if needed

DIRECTIONS

In a medium bowl, using an electric mixer,
cream the margarine and shortening
together. Add the vanilla and blend.
Incorporate the powdered sugar 1 cup at
a time, mixing well, until the frosting is
firm but spreadable and has your desired
sweetness. If the buttercream is not as
smooth as you would like, add the milk.

CHOCOLATE BUTTERCREAM

Makes: 1½ cups

INGREDIENTS

1/4 cup
chocolate chips,
melted and cooled

1/2 cup
margarine, at room temperature

2 to 3 cups
powdered sugar

2 tablespoons
baking cocoa

1 to 2 tablespoons
nondairy milk

DIRECTIONS

In a medium bowl, using an electric
mixer, cream together the chocolate
and margarine until smooth. In another
bowl, sift the powdered sugar and cocoa
powder together. Add 2 cups of the sugar
mixture to the chocolate mixture and beat
well, then add more until the frosting is
firm but spreadable and has your desired
sweetness. Add the milk and mix until firm
but smooth and spreadable.

MATCHA BUTTERCREAM
Makes: 1 1/2 cups

INGREDIENTS

1/2 cup
margarine, at room temperature

1 1/2 teaspoons
matcha powder

1 tablespoon
nondairy milk

1/4 teaspoon
vanilla extract

2 to 3 cups
powdered sugar, sifted

DIRECTIONS

In a large bowl, using an electric mixer, cream the margarine. In a small bowl, dissolve the matcha powder in the milk. Add the matcha mixture and vanilla to the margarine and mix well. Incorporate the powdered sugar 1 cup at a time, mixing well, until the frosting is firm but spreadable and has your desired sweetness.

COFFEE BUTTERCREAM
Makes: 1 1/2 cups

INGREDIENTS

1/4 cup
margarine, at room temperature

1/4 cup
shortening or margarine, at room temperature

1/2 to 1 teaspoon
instant coffee granules, depending on desired intensity of flavor

1 tablespoon
nondairy milk

2 to 3 cups
powdered sugar, sifted

DIRECTIONS

In a medium bowl, using an electric mixer, cream together the margarine and shortening until combined. Dissolve the coffee in the milk and beat into the margarine mixture. Add the powdered sugar, 1 cup at a time, until the frosting is firm but spreadable and has your desired sweetness.

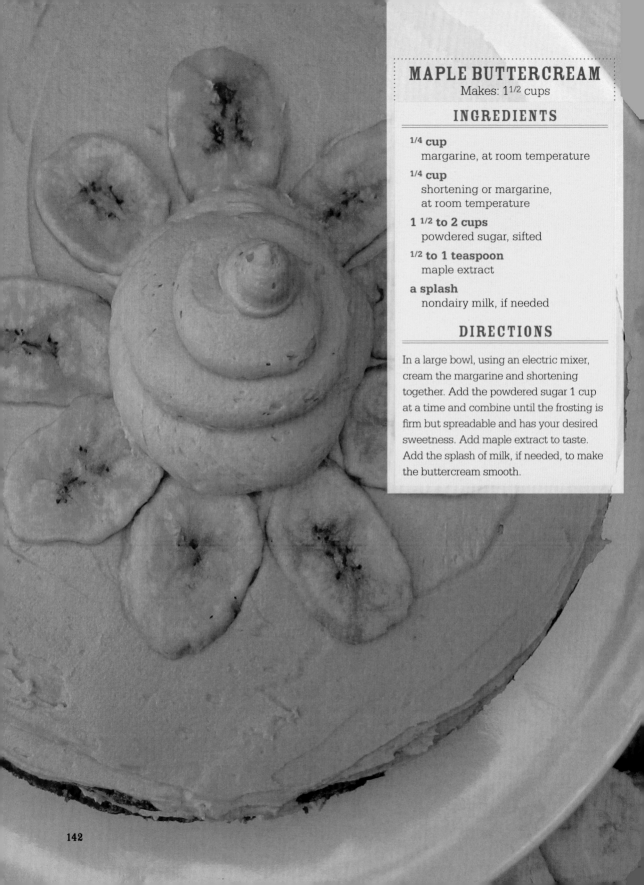

MAPLE BUTTERCREAM
Makes: 1 1/2 cups

INGREDIENTS

1/4 cup
margarine, at room temperature

1/4 cup
shortening or margarine,
at room temperature

1 1/2 to 2 cups
powdered sugar, sifted

1/2 to 1 teaspoon
maple extract

a splash
nondairy milk, if needed

DIRECTIONS

In a large bowl, using an electric mixer,
cream the margarine and shortening
together. Add the powdered sugar 1 cup
at a time and combine until the frosting is
firm but spreadable and has your desired
sweetness. Add maple extract to taste.
Add the splash of milk, if needed, to make
the buttercream smooth.

INDEX

ABOUT THE AUTHOR

KRIS HOLECHEK is a vegan baker, blogger, and recipe formulating mad scientist. She is the author of *The Damn Tasty! Vegan Baking Guide* and *The 100 Best Vegan Baking Recipes*, and the writer of www.nomnomnomblog .com. She lives in Eugene, Oregon, with her husband, cats, and a self-admittedly ridiculous amount of kitchen gadgets.